Redefining Diva

Redefining Diva

SHERYL LEE RALPH

HUNTER

GALLERY BOOKS | KAREN HUNTER PUBLISHING

New York   London   Toronto   Sydney   New Delhi

G

Gallery Books
A Division of Simon & Schuster, Inc.
1230 Avenue of the Americas
New York, NY 10020

HUNTER

Karen Hunter Publishing
A Division of Suitt-Hunter Enterprises, LLC
598 Broadway, 3rd Floor
New York, NY 10012

First Karen Hunter Publishing/Gallery Books trade paperback edition March 2012

GALLERY and colophon are registered trademarks of Simon & Schuster, Inc.

For information about special discounts for bulk purchases, please contact Simon & Schuster Special Sales at 1-866-506-1949 or business@simonandschuster.com.

The Simon & Schuster Speakers Bureau can bring authors to your live event. For more information or to book an event, contact the Simon & Schuster Speakers Bureau at 1-866-248-3049 or visit our website at www.simonspeakers.com.

Designed by Akasha Archer

Manufactured in the United States of America

10 9 8 7 6 5

Library of Congress Cataloging-in-Publication Data is available.

ISBN 978-1-4516-0842-7
ISBN 978-1-4516-0881-6 (ebook)

This book is dedicated to some of the biggest Divinely Inspired Victoriously Alive DIVA people I know—my family!

My parents, Dr. Stanley and Miss Ivy, you have weathered the storms of life and have come out on the other side together in the calm of victory! I thank you for every sacrifice you have made and continue to make so that your family continues to prosper. If prayers and faith will secure us a place in heaven, then I know we are all taken care of!

To my brothers, Stanley, Timmy, and Michael, thank you for acknowledging that I am the captain of the ship and "a good one"! We charted a life course together and I couldn't have a better crew than the three of you.

To my children, Etienne and Coco, I look at you and know that I have done something wonderful in my life because after I am gone I will leave two outstanding human beings to take my place. Continue to make me proud. I love you in ways you will never completely understand.

Miss Mae, it was God who sent you to our family. You have loved and cared for my children as if they were your own and kept my home together. What a blessing you are.

Finally and so importantly, I thank my husband, Vincent, one of the most divinely inspired, victoriously anointed Diva men I know. Senator, I will always be your first lady. You came into my life right in the nick of time, and that has made all the difference for me. Your strength, love, and wisdom bless me indeed.

Wonderful, what can I say but wonderful.
Yes, it's wonderful.
Tonight has been so wonderful and new.
And I couldn't have done it alone, I thank you.

—"Press Conference" from *Dreamgirls*

Contents

Author's Note ✳ xiii

INTRODUCTION ✳ xv
How I Became a Diva

CHAPTER ONE ✳ 1
Discover Your Diva Legacy

CHAPTER TWO ✳ 15
A Diva Finds Her Joy

CHAPTER THREE ✳ 27
A Diva Takes Risks

CHAPTER FOUR ✳ 45
A Diva Fights for Her Dreams

CHAPTER FIVE ✳ 57
A Diva Doesn't Quit

CHAPTER SIX ✳ 67

A Diva Embraces the Chaos

CHAPTER SEVEN ✳ 77

A Diva Gets Her Dream

CHAPTER EIGHT ✳ 83

A Diva Struggles

CHAPTER NINE ✳ 97

A Diva Deals with Difficult People

CHAPTER TEN ✳ 105

A Diva Has Good Days . . . and Bad Ones

CHAPTER ELEVEN ✳ 119

Divas Have Growing Pains Too

CHAPTER TWELVE ✳ 131

Divahood Ain't Always Easy

CHAPTER THIRTEEN ✳ 139

A Diva Knows When to Make an Exit

CHAPTER FOURTEEN ✳ 155

A Diva Takes Risks

CHAPTER FIFTEEN ✳ 171

No Diva, No Problems

CHAPTER SIXTEEN ✶ 183

A Diva Looks Back . . . and Forward

AN EPILOGUE . . . ✶ 195

The Diva's Final Chapter

Acknowledgments ✶ 199

Author's Note

It is important to note that *Diva* is more than just big hair and attitude for me. A *Diva* is an acronym: *Divinely Inspired Victoriously Anointed.* A *Diva* is *Definitely Inspirational and Vivaciously Alive.* *Divas* are *Daringly Inquisitive and Valiantly Aware.* Create your own *Diva* and embrace it. You will never know the *Diva* you are until you do. And when you do, you will laugh out loud and dance with your *Diva* self, knowing that you too are *Divinely Inspired Victoriously Alive!*

Be inwardly gorgeous and outwardly fabulous, *Diva!*

INTRODUCTION

How I Became a Diva

I am *the Ultimate Diva.* At least, that's what they tell me. I have been called *Diva* on TV shows and in magazines. I have been called *Diva* by close friends and utter strangers. I have been called every kind of Diva you can imagine, from *Renaissance Diva* to *Warrior Diva. Real-Life Diva* to *Queen Diva,* and my favorite, *Diva-licious.* I've heard it more times than I can count: *Sheryl Lee Ralph is a true Diva.*

And to them I say, *Thank you.*

Being called a Diva used to bother me a lot. People love to throw around the D-word, and most times it's synonymous with the B-word. Whether you spell *witch* with a *w* or a *b,* that is not me. When most people hear the word *Diva* to describe a woman, the first thing that pops into their mind is big hair and an even bigger, badder attitude. And there certainly are Divas that fit the bill.

You know them: an A-list celebrity finds her collection of Louis Vuitton luggage in the wrong order, she pitches a fit, throws her BlackBerry at the nearest assistant and ends up in court and on the cover of *People* magazine. "What a *Diva!*" says the press.

Then there's the young "actress" on her first film who refuses to leave her trailer because craft services forgot to stock her favorite brand of bottled water and white M&M's! So in playing the role of Diva—and she has been painfully miscast—she holds up filming for three hours. When she finally gets to the set, she doesn't know her lines. But there are no consequences for her when she's offered the film sequel and her own reality show. *Diva-in-Training*.

And then there is the *Wannabe Diva*. You probably know a few of these Divas yourself. They aren't easy to miss. They are usually loud and rude, with a touch of violence thrown in for bad measure. The *Wannabe Diva* wouldn't hesitate to steal your parking spot or your man. And she'll go for both without so much as an *I'm sorry* or *Excuse me*. You can love her or hate her and it won't make a bit of difference, 'cause she doesn't care what you think about anything!

Divas, according to public perception, are egotistical, self-centered, high-maintenance, spoiled little brats. But here is the truth, my friends: none of the aforementioned women are *true Divas*. These women give *Diva* a bad name. A real Diva—the kind who makes you sit up and take notice in a good way—is a woman of strength, character, and a beauty that radiates from within. She copies no one. She is her own woman.

My kind of Diva has a voice and uses it to speak her mind, understanding that inner thoughts don't always need to be outer thoughts. She loves herself. She believes in herself enough to respect herself. But disrespect herself and others by pitching hissy fits, fighting, cursing, and throwing things at people? Not my Diva. A true Diva woman would never waste her time or stoop to the lows of acting like a petty, nasty B-word. A real Diva gets what she wants because people *want* to give it to her. A real Diva demands respect by *respecting herself and others.*

But when and why did the term *Diva* turn into an insult? To find the answer you have to take a look into the past, because any Diva worth her salt pays respect to her legacy.

Some believe the term *Diva* originated in opera two centuries ago. Diva was used to describe the classic self-centered Prima Donna, storming off the stage with a cry of "Call me when you get it together!" These women were notorious for creating chaos and confusion. The Prima Donna lived for drama. These women would have frightened the daylights out of the likes of a little *Wannabe Diva.* And they wouldn't have to say a word to do it!

But when you dig deeper to discover the origins of Diva, you find that the word became part of the English language in the late-nineteenth century to describe a woman of *extraordinary gifts and talent. Diva* comes from the Italian noun for a female deity, which is derived from the Latin word *divus.* And diva translates to *goddess.* That's right. At her very roots, *the Diva is a goddess. Of course she is!*

A Diva is divine. She is, after all, a *goddess.*

A Diva is nothing if not inspiring!

A Diva is victorious.

A Diva is anointed. She is a chosen woman.

A Diva looks in the mirror and loves what she sees. She knows that she has to take care of that woman staring back at her. She knows the truth: *if you don't love yourself, how in the world are you going to love anyone else?* My kind of Diva is woman enough to love herself to the core of her being. Those women cussing, fussing, and fighting anyone who dares look at them sideways? Fakes, phonies, and pure imposters! My kind of Diva has better things to do . . . like improve herself and her community. She respects herself and those around her. She is a role model. My kind of Diva is changing the world in big and small ways. *And, yes, she looks good doing it.*

I never set out to be divine or inspiring. I never knew I'd be chosen for the role of Diva. I believe that I am the *Accidental Diva.* But when young women come up and tell me I inspire them to own their talent and strength? Well, I say, if that's the kind of Diva woman you see me as, then *I am all right with that!*

I'm often asked how I became a Diva. Well, I had good teachers. All Divas have a Diva mentor or the "auntie in her head." And if you don't have one, you need to search one out. I had many Diva mentors in my head growing up: Diahann Carroll, so beautiful and well-spoken; Miriam Makeba, a singer and revolutionary from South Africa; Yvonne Brathwaite Burke—groundbreaking politician and mother; Diana Ross and every single one of the Supremes. I mean, I secretly wanted to grow up and dye my hair "Mary Wilson blond."

And then there was Nina Simone.

Nina Simone was a bold soul sistah and there was nothing conventional about her. She was a real rule breaker and what I call an *obvious black woman.* If you are two shades darker than Halle Berry, a lot of people might say that you are *too dark* or *too black.* Miss Nina Simone was at least three shades darker than Halle Berry, living in a time when many people considered "black" anything but beautiful.

Nina Simone came to that Diva moment when she yanked off her wig and sang out, "To be young, gifted and black is where it's at!" I remember hearing that song on the radio, and something changed for me. I was empowered by the words. I was changed, just as Diva Nina had changed. She recreated herself.

I had seen earlier pictures of her posing in those sequined, body-clinging dresses and huge wigs "Negro" women of a certain time wore. Somehow, they always looked more like a hat to me. But when "To Be Young, Gifted and Black" came out on the *Black Gold* album, the cover made a real statement. There was a silhouette of Diva Nina, who had now gone natural, sporting a short Afro, big earrings, and an African dashiki. She looked so comfortable in her skin. It was as if she were saying, *I am what I am and there is nothing wrong with me. I am black, I am beautiful, and there is no reason for me to hide . . . anything. Not even my natural hair.*

Ms. Simone was one of the first black female artists to go natural, followed by Aretha Franklin and Roberta Flack, and that summer, much to the shock of my parents, so did I. I was at one with Ms. Simone whenever she opened her mouth to share that gorgeous voice. She'd wail and moan singing those songs of protest and her own kind of peace. She sang in a way that made you say, *That is a proud black woman right there. An African woman, and that woman is beautiful. DIVA.*

What an impression she made on me.

I believe that God orders your steps from the day you are born, and he later ordered my steps to the south of France

XX   *Introduction*

and to a dinner honoring Gregory Peck during the Cannes Film Festival. I took my seat in the lavishly decorated room with the white flowers and candles and a table set for royalty. When I looked up, sitting right in front of me was the Diva, Ms. Nina Simone. She was older now and in a wheelchair, but she was still beautiful with that lovely black skin that refused to crack.

I immediately got up from my seat and walked over to her. I said, "Excuse me, but you're Nina Simone," and she looked up at me with a huge white smile and proudly said, "Yes, I am." We talked briefly about *Dreamgirls* and shared mutual moments of adoration. I could hardly believe I was talking to her. She was wearing a turban, pearls, and a vibrant yellow silk dress. She was charming and still outspoken. Yes, she'd had controversy in her life—there was always the story about how she carried a small gun in her purse and wasn't afraid to pull it out. Yes, she'd had failures and a few broken hearts. But like any true Diva, she was never one to lie down and roll over during hard times. She had learned that mistakes often turn into great successes. True Divas never just survive . . . they *thrive*.

When Nina Simone said she was proud of me, she had no idea what she was doing for the little girl she inspired to cut off her hair, put gloss on her full lips and say to the world, *This is who I am!* The Diva I am today exists because fearless women who came before would not let the world define them.

And that is why I am writing this book. Because of Divas such as Nina Simone, Gran Ma Becky, Nana, Mrs. Brown, Auntie Carolyn, Rosalind Cash, Virginia Capers, Susan Taylor . . . and, of course, my mother.

They were the kind of woman I wanted to be—strong,

proud, and full of purpose. They fought the odds and just kept going. They inspired me just by being themselves and loving me.

I hope, after you finish reading this book, you too will be inspired. I hope that someone calls you *Diva* and you lift your head, open your heart, and respond by saying, "Thank you."

1

Discover Your Diva Legacy

When Broadway history is being made, you can feel it, read the *New York Times* on December 21, 1981.

And that was just the beginning.

That was the review I woke up to that wintry morning in New York after the opening-night performance of *Dreamgirls* on Broadway. It had been a long, rough road, but that single review opened the floodgates of fame. There would be television appearances and Tony nominations. My picture would grace the pages of *Vogue, Bazaar, Glamour, Essence,* and the cover of *Ebony.* People would offer body parts to be signed—and *most* of them I signed with a smile. The tiny dressing room I shared with Loretta Devine would overflow with flowers, telegrams, and gifts. My first Louis Vuitton handbag, a gift from a drag queen; a vertical record player from Rick James; a bottle of perfume sent from Diane von Fürstenberg herself. Backstage visits from Sly Stallone, Michael Jackson, Luther Vandross, people I'd only heard on the radio or seen from the seat of my local movie theater.

Overnight I'd gone from being just another struggling actress pounding the pavement with a movie and a few TV shows under my belt, to being loved and adored by perfect strangers in the theater and on the street. Night after night the audiences rose to their feet and showered us with the kind of applause that lets you know you are loved . . . *really, truly loved*. God it felt *good*!

Overnight, along with my castmates, I had become the toast of the town—the belle of the ball on Broadway—and my life would forever be changed. If you had told me what was in store, I would never have believed you. If you'd told me that decades later there would be a *Dreamgirls* movie with a great young star cast in a role I had created, singing songs and saying lines I'd help write . . . or that Diana Ross would find ways *not* to speak to me . . . or that anyone would ever associate my name with a word like *Diva* in the same way they did Miss Ross . . . well, I'd have thought you were just plain crazy. But most of all, I *would not* have signed away my creative rights to *Dreamgirls* for a *single US dollar*.

I was young and dumb and loving the job I was doing. I was living my dream, stepping out under those bright lights every night and singing my heart out and looking good.

I was only twenty-four, after all.

My mother also faced some of her greatest challenges at the age of twenty-four. That was the year in which she first came to the United States with the dream of getting a job, going to school to become a nurse, and buying a house.

"Don't let life frighten you," my mother would say in her melodious Jamaican accent.

Travel back then was expensive and someone had to

sponsor you. It was a long trip from Jamaica, and because of the cost, most island immigrants flew to Miami then took the train to New York. My mother's aunt Maude had sent for her, and she was expecting her money back.

My mother found work in Harlem Hospital as a nurse's aide so that she could repay Aunt Maude. To this day, my mother doesn't like to owe anybody anything, especially money. She enrolled in night school to further her dream of education but dropped out after only three weeks in America when she met my father. He was a student at NYU doing his master's and working nights as a hospital operator. My mother said that the very first time she heard his voice over the loudspeaker, she just *had to meet him*. And that was that!

What makes this story even more special is that during that time in the fifties, there was a separation between black Americans and West Indians. American blacks used to call West Indians "monkey chasers," "coconut," and other vicious names. It's sad to think about, but there were West Indian *dreams* and an American *reality*. So many groups stayed to themselves, but not my mother. She heard that American voice and *she was going to meet him* and *introduce herself to him*. Her life was changed by not being afraid of rejection or anything else.

My grandmother on my father's side was born in the summer of 1910 and was never frightened by life either. Nana never let anyone tell her what she could or could not do. As a young girl, she was considered one of the most beautiful girls in her small, dusty North Carolina town. Like any of the other young ladies of the time, she could cook, sew, and was active in her church. After Sunday dinner, she would sit knitting on the front porch with her sisters and mother. Young men would pass in the distance, since the house was set far back off the road. They would tip their hats hoping for some sort of acknowledgment, but these belles would barely acknowledge the many suitors passing for a glimpse. *If I liked one,* she used to tell me, *I might give them a tiny nod, but never a wave. You would never yell hello or offer any conversation. That just wasn't ladylike. Besides, you never talked to any young man you hadn't been formally introduced to.*

My grandmother helped teach me the value of politeness. She believed that manners really mattered, especially for a pretty "Negro." With real manners she could be respected. Nana also taught me that you could be a lady and still have your own mind. In her time, most believed marriage was a woman's only option for financial stability, but my grandmother never let anyone tell her what to believe. She had her own thoughts and beliefs.

My grandmother had caught the attention of a rather "fancy" man in her town and she was not thrilled. Most women would have welcomed the attention, but not my grandmother. She didn't like him, much less love him. But beyond that, she wanted something more for herself. She'd read somewhere about factories up North looking to hire Negro workers. Unemployed Negroes would gather in certain parts of town and were offered bus tickets to work in factory cities such as Chicago, New York, and Detroit. Being a true old-school Diva herself, my grandmother—the youngest of eight—decided there was more out there in the world to explore. So without telling anyone, she accepted a one-way bus ticket, packed her bag full of dreams, and headed north.

My grandmother was a true Diva in the best sense of the word. She passed this fearlessness on to me. A lifetime later, that same fearlessness gave me the guts to find my way to Hollywood.

I remember calling my father from a phone booth at the Los Angeles airport. I hadn't even collected my luggage. I just found the nearest phone and dialed.

"Daddy?" I said.

"Sheryl Lee Ralph," he said, using all three of my names in a way that let me know I was in trouble, "where are you?"

"California."

"What are you doing in California?" he asked, completely dumbfounded.

I didn't have an answer because I wasn't sure myself. I'd just landed in the United States after completing a tour of duty with the Department of Defense. With a government-issued rank of GS-12, I was the singing "bodyguard" for the *Penthouse* Pet of the Year. I'll never forget all the servicemen holding up their open *Penthouse* magazines asking, *Which one are you?* I was only nineteen, and still a bit on the innocent side. Embarrassed as I was, I had to tell them that I was there to sing. Some were disappointed as they knew what they wanted to see, but others were all smiles after hearing what my voice could do. One man—I'll never forget him—simply looked at me and said, "I'm glad you're not in the magazine."

Performances for the armed forces were some of the best times in my life. To this day I have a great fondness for those who serve our country. It is a great sacrifice. They could be a tough audience but they always loved you for just showing up for them. And it was a great experience for a Diva-in-training. I had traveled halfway around the world seeing places and things many people just imagined seeing. Uncle Sam took very good care of me. But now my tour of duty was over and I had to return to New York, with a stopover in San Francisco or Los Angeles. I didn't have to think twice; I chose LA.

So there I was at LAX, a nineteen-year-old fresh out of college, trying to be a singer-slash-actress. A girl who'd gotten off the plane, left her luggage behind, and was now calling home because she had no idea where to go or how to achieve her dreams.

My father was not thrilled. "You better get back on that plane and come home! Come home now."

"Daddy, you know I'm coming home, but not yet. Right now I have to be here."

"What in heaven's name are you going to do?"

"I don't know yet."

My father sighed. My father knew firsthand just how stubborn I could be when I'd made up my mind about something. I knew my future was in LA, and I was going to be a star. All the soldiers had told me that and I just *knew*. What I didn't know? Where I'd be sleeping that night.

"Well," said my father, knowing I couldn't be convinced otherwise, "believe it or not, I just hung up the phone with my cousin Mabel. I haven't spoken to her in years, and she just happened to call me long-distance."

"Mabel?"

"Yes. And you'll never believe where she lives."

* * *

Just like my mother and grandmother, I was not afraid to take a risk. And that is another lesson I learned from them: any *divinely inspired, virtuously anointed* woman knows that you *have* to take risks. Yes, you are bound to make mistakes . . . but *mistake* is just another word for *experience*. Enough experience often adds up to success.

Eventually, my grandmother married. He wasn't the richest man, but she didn't care because in the end she married for love. My grandfather was a good man. A bit on the quiet side, he was a great sportsman, hunter, and athlete. He loved taking me to dog shows and tennis matches. He was a talented golfer, but never got the chance to really enjoy the fairways simply because of the color of his skin. He'd caddy for white men to get the chance to play a few rounds himself. He could fix anything, including people.

With the support of a good woman—and any real Diva woman inspires her man to be the best he can be—my grandfather went on to help countless young people in the community. He developed after-school tennis programs for students because he felt that an "idle mind is the devil's workshop." And he was right.

In the end, my grandfather was murdered in our family home by an intruder. The young man who did it was a part of the athletic program my grandfather had created for youth in need.

And my grandmother stood beside my grandfather right until the end.

Not until much later in her life did she finally tell me a bit about that night: "He just bled out. I tried to hold the blood back, hold his insides together, but it was too late. I screamed but it was like no one could hear me. Like there was a veil over us and the house. I held him and just watched the life leave him. Then he was gone."

It was a crisp Wednesday evening in September when the boys came to rob the house. Wednesday was Bible study, so they figured everyone would be at church. They expected an empty home, but that night my grandparents had left church early because my grandmother wasn't feeling well.

My grandmother saw the back door was open and entered the house. She grabbed a kitchen knife and she went after the thieves. When I was younger, I often wondered what she was thinking at that moment. But now, I think I know . . . not only was she defending her husband, but she was also defending herself. She was defending the life she loved. She was defending all those years she'd struggled to make a comfortable home for her family, put three kids through college, and one through the army.

My grandmother was a fighter. She lunged for one of the boys, but before the knife could reach him, my grandfather had been shot with a double-barrel shotgun point-blank to the chest.

I often wonder what would have happened if my grandmother had not gone after that boy, but that wasn't her way. Like any real Diva, my grandmother stayed true to herself. She would go to any lengths to protect those that she loved, including putting herself in danger even if it killed her.

My grandmother survived, but not before she too was shot. My grandmother Julia—the most beautiful woman in her

North Carolina town—was shot right in the face. She was scarred forever, both physically and emotionally. But she did what she had to do and passed that strength on to me. I've always been told I'm very much like her, and for that I am forever grateful.

Years later, I'd love watching the TV show *Julia.* Seeing my grandmother's name splashed across the screen brought back memories of her fortitude. One of my daughter's names is Julia, and I hope this is a reminder to her of the current of strength running through our lineage and veins.

My grandmother was so proud of my being on Broadway. She had always had a dream to sing and dance like Josephine Baker, Florence Mills, or Bessie Smith. But it wasn't the kind of career a real lady pursued if she had options. Showing your legs—much less your cleavage—was socially unacceptable and certainly unladylike. Everybody knew that the life of a showgirl could lead to tragedy as the use of drugs and alcohol were common. My grandmother chose marriage and kept her singing to the church choir.

During my run on Broadway in *Dreamgirls,* I often called my grandmother before a show. Nothing made her happier than those calls from the theater. *Who was in the audience? Who had I met? Was I eating to keep up my strength 'cause you had to be strong to be really famous.* Wow, was she right.

My grandmother changed gradually after the shooting. Sometimes she'd be cheerful, sipping her favorite scotch, and sometimes she'd seem distant and somewhere far away. But the request never changed: "Sing a li'l song for me, Sheryl Lee," she'd say. "Sing a li'l song for me."

I'm still singing for my grandmother. Every time I open my

mouth—whether on a Broadway stage or for my husband and children—I sing for her. I sing for my mother and the strong women who came before me . . . the ones who shaped me to be the woman I am today. These are my Diva mentors, and the women I look to for strength when I feel as though the weight of my world is too much to carry.

I was blessed to have a wonderful grandmother and mother. Two women different as day and night, but they both loved me deeply and unconditionally, strengthening me with life lessons that continue to guide me. But we aren't all blessed that way. Perhaps your mother was unavailable. Maybe she had life issues or wasn't around much, or you never met her in the first place. Does that mean you won't have your own Diva mentor? A real Diva-in-training won't let that stop her.

I have been blessed with the support and mentorship of some of the most wonderful and giving women God ever created. Some of these women found me, but others I sought out on my own. You never know when a Diva mentor will come into your life, so keep your eyes open for her arrival.

When I was thirteen, I met Susan Taylor on summer vacation in Jamaica. My mother's design salon kept me in contact with the "who's who" of visitors to the island. My mom's friend, Pat Ramsey, and her brilliant photographer husband, Ken, knew a young, vibrant model. I remember the first time I saw her—bald head, big eyes, and huge hoop earrings—and I was as smitten as any little girl would be when face-to-face with a beautiful big girl. There is an iconic picture of Susan Taylor taken by Mr. Ramsey in which she is looking over her shoulder. In my young mind I imagined her looking right at me saying, "You coming?"

I have followed Susan Taylor to some degree my whole career, emulating her grace and kindness. She is a Queen Diva!

At the age of fifteen, during another summer in Jamaica, I met Rosalind "Roz" Cash, whom I knew to be a great actress. Roz took me under her wing and encouraged my dreams. Originally from New Jersey, she sometimes visited me at Rutgers University, always causing a stir with her handsome companion and green Mercedes. She encouraged my education in school and onstage. She helped in securing my audition for the Negro Ensemble Company's actor training program and was so proud of my acceptance. She opened her home to me when I needed a place to stay in Los Angeles. Roz remained supportive up until her untimely death of cancer.

I met Virginia Capers at the age of nineteen when I was chosen as one of the Top Ten College Women in America by *Glamour* magazine. With that award, I was to join an elite group of women that included Martha Stewart. The greatest gift was that I was given the opportunity to meet "a woman of influence" in my chosen field. I chose Tony Award winner for *Raisin in the Sun* "Aunt" Virginia Capers, who immediately embraced me like her own child. She helped me set goals and deadlines in my career and encouraged me as I crossed every finish line. She sat front and center when I performed in community theater and was there for the premieres of *A Piece of the Action* and *Dreamgirls*. She was proud as any mother when I was nominated for the Tony Award and told me that she "wasn't surprised." Aunt Virginia made sure my first apartment was "suitable" by finding it for me. She always shared her showbiz war stories with me and always encouraged me to take the higher road because, according to her, "the same a** you kick today, you may have to kiss tomorrow."

I keep her picture at my front door so she will always see me in my comings and goings. I miss and love her!

Even Elizabeth Taylor, whom I did not know as long or as well, was a wealth of support as I branched out speaking about AIDS. Another quick-witted woman, she told me not to be disheartened by those who tried to bring me down. "Don't let those people stop you," she said. "Most of them couldn't find their a** if it wasn't connected to them!"

These women made a deep and unforgettable mark on my life as a woman and a performer. And there are women out there who will do the same for you. A real Diva finds her Diva mentors. She seeks them out. A real Diva—the kind you want to be—looks to the women who came before her to inspire her.

So next time you feel overwhelmed and think you have nowhere to turn, remember the women who paved the way for you. Search for the Diva around you. Maybe you know her personally—in your church or at your school. Maybe you've heard her on the radio—your local politician or entrepreneur. Maybe you've only read about her in books and magazines—the celebrity or actress. *They all have lessons to teach you.*

Just as my grandmother and mother gave me strength, your Diva mentor can do the same for you. With the right Diva mentor you will find a wise and trusted guide and adviser. A woman who serves as a role model just by living. Look to her for guidance, and you will not believe the heights to which you will rise.

2

A Diva Finds Her Joy

When I was growing up, my mother always used to tell me, "Be a doctor, be a lawyer. And if you can't do that, then marry one!" I knew better than to argue with a strong West Indian woman once she'd made up her mind.

No matter what she said, I knew my mother only wanted what she felt was best for me. I had parents who did their best when it came to loving me, making sure I had a good education. Even more, they made sure I felt good about myself, no matter how funny looking I was. And I was truly funny looking.

That self-esteem my parents built inside me is probably what kept me from being afraid when, at sixteen, I entered my freshman year of college at Rutgers University in the first class that accepted women. Rutgers had historically been a male university, and when greater minds prevailed, opening its doors to women, only two African-Americans were in that class. Of those two young women, I was the youngest.

Looking back, I should have been terrified. I should have had a million doubts in my mind. *What will they think of me? Will I fit in? Will I be able to handle the course load?* But I wasn't frightened or nervous, I was excited. And I never doubted that I belonged at that illustrious institution. My parents had taught me the value of hard work, and I knew I'd earned my place there just like the great Paul Robeson.

Besides, I had goals and I was determined to meet them. If anyone ever thought I didn't belong, well, I didn't notice. I was determined to succeed. I wanted to make a name for myself in this world. I wanted to be a successful, respected . . . *doctor.*

That was the only part that didn't feel quite right.

I knew I could perform. I'd been singing, dancing, and acting since I was a child. The year before I'd entered college I had participated in the Miss Black Teenage America Pageant in New York. I wasn't dreaming about the golden statue and sparkling crown as much as I was dreaming about that scholarship check they gave the winner. My talent was singing and acting; those were things I knew I could do well. Even after taking home the 1st Runner-Up title and a $5,000 scholarship, which, much to my father's delight, paid for almost two years of college, it never occurred to me that I could sing and dance *for a living.*

But I had no idea about destiny when I started at Rutgers. I had other things to think about, like a packed class schedule.

Of course, a true Diva can't escape her destiny.

I will never forget my first day of Organic Chemistry. I was presented with a hare and a scalpel. There it was, a dead rabbit in front of me. I was expected to open it up with that shiny new instrument. *I don't think so!* I gave that scalpel back to the instructor and told them that this was the first and last time they would see me. I left that class knowing that I was not going to be a doctor and immediately went over to the registrar's office to see if I could find a course that would help me to become a lawyer.

Constitutional Law essentially encompasses all the foundational laws that our country is based upon, and that is a whole lot of laws! I sat in that class and I was miserable. The teacher who taught the class was a small, tightly wound woman with glasses and a severe bun. She never smiled. Her speech was like chalk screeching on the blackboard, real chalk screeching too. I had to get out of there, so I left that class just like the other.

So there I was walking across the campus after leaving Constitutional Law class. It was a drab, gray day and I felt drab and gray too. Little Sheryl Lee Ralph, college girl who had found freedom in jeans and golden platform shoes, her Afro and textbooks loaded into her sharp African-textile book bag, was having a *complete and utter meltdown*. I knew the world was full of excitement and inspiration, and I knew I wasn't going to find either of those things in Organic Chemistry or Constitutional Law! I was not going to become a doctor or a lawyer. How could I possibly tell my mother that? In my first month of college it was clear that I was not going to be able to live up to her dream of me becoming a doctor or a lawyer, and I wasn't even thinking about marrying one.

Back in the day, many women went to college to find their husband. Many of my good friends met their future spouse while at Rutgers. But I knew that early marriage wasn't for me either. I was younger than my classmates, and the idea of finding a husband, starting a family, and giving up my dreams? No way.

Just like my grandmother, I knew my own dreams had to

come first. The only problem: I just wasn't quite sure what those dreams were yet.

I wandered the campus, thinking, *How am I goin' to tell Mother?* The thought of her reaction to my revelation filled me with dread. I didn't want to hear her mouth after I broke the news. Somehow, as I wandered, I ended up in front of a theater. Fate? Maybe. My subconscious leading me there? More likely.

And hanging on the front door of the theater was a sign: AUDITIONS TODAY.

I didn't think twice. I practically flew right into that auditorium and signed up to audition. I had my monologue and song from the Miss Black Teenage America Pageant, and I was ready to use them.

Dr. John Bettenbender was a gruff-looking, older man with a long beard who smoked a pipe. He was the head—king, really—of the Theater Department and everybody knew it. Except me, of course. He looked up at me from his seat—surrounded by a large cloud of smoke—and bellowed, "Who are you?"

"Sheryl Lee Ralph," I said. "And I would like to audition."

"Well," he grumbled, looking at me over his glasses, "get on the stage, then."

I dropped my bag of legal textbooks and was onstage so fast it made my *own* head spin. But I found my home the moment I took my place center stage.

I had no idea what I was doing, but what I was doing felt so good and so right.

Dr. Bettenbender just looked at me and kept smoking that pipe of his. I took a deep breath, opened my mouth, and performed my monologue, which I had written myself. I followed it up with an a cappella version of "Summertime." That little speech and song had gotten me first runner-up in the pageant, and it also got me the king's attention.

After being confronted with having to cut up the Easter bunny, and sitting through that boring law class, and the realization that the worlds of Doctor and Attorney would not be mine, in that moment of auditioning I felt completely alive. Right there on that stage, I felt whole. I felt as though I had found myself, and I am so grateful for that.

There is a Diva lesson in all this: *when you find your joy and are doing what you are meant to do, you'll know it. Everything will feel right.*

When I finished my audition, Dr. Bettenbender was silent for quite a while with that pipe smoke around his head. Finally he opened his mouth. "What did you say your name was?"

"Sheryl Lee Ralph."

"Well, Sheryl Lee Ralph," he said. "You just got yourself cast."

Just like that, I could see my whole future spread out before me . . . and I liked what I saw. My future was on the stage, not in a courtroom and certainly *not* in the operating room, and I felt utter relief.

I spent that year acting in musicals and plays, taking acting classes, meeting other actors, learning my craft, and looking forward to the new challenge each day would bring me. I began to see that this joy I had discovered—the ability to entertain—could actually become a career . . . *my* career. I might actually make money doing *what I loved*. That thought filled me with elation and hope . . . not to mention *fear*.

Yes, I was afraid. *How would I do it, this acting thing? How would I survive?* But most of all, *what about my parents?* My parents loved me, adored me. They sacrificed to give me the gift of an exceptional education at one of the nation's leading universities and made sure that there were always hands to lift me when I fell. How could I disappoint them? Not to mention, I wasn't exactly picking the most stable career path. All those things I was taught that good parents do for their children—take them to church, keep them clothed and fed and safe—would I be able to do that for my future children . . . if I even had any? Actresses worry about keeping their bodies in shape and their minds free of the responsibilities of other people, right? If I followed this path, would my community respect me? I had no idea. My mind was a mess of conflicting emotions.

Then I'd go onstage, and everything made sense.

I often meet young women who hate their jobs. They don't like the people they work with and don't like what they do. Had I gone in another direction, I'd be just like them, unhappy. Making everyone around me unhappy. Wondering why I can't find and keep a good relationship. Here's what I tell those women: if you are working at something, and it isn't making you happy, well, you need to find yourself another job. If you don't find your work fulfilling, well, *you need to find yourself another job.* If you don't wake up in the morning with a feeling that you just can't wait to get to work and be the best you can possibly be, well, you probably know what I'm going to say to that.

If you take a job just to have a job, then you aren't really living. You are just surviving, not thriving. Now don't get me wrong, sometimes a Diva has to do what a Diva has to do to put food on the table, but she knows to find her joy at all costs. Because *a real Diva thrives.*

There are a million reasons and excuses to keep you from finding your joy and the work that fulfills you. The uncertainty of stepping out on faith alone. The fear of rejection, people telling you that it is impossible because it hasn't been possible for them. Others thinking that you have lost your mind or are just plain crazy. Which leads you to think, *What about the rent? What about my hair, my nails, my designer morning latte?* All those things cost money, honey. So what are you going to do? Are you going to lie down and roll over with the daily unhappiness and say, *Well, I guess that's it?* Of course not. You're a Diva, and any real Diva is willing to rise to the challenge of her own life.

Well, Miss Diva, you might be thinking, *That's easy for you to say.* Listen, I didn't get to where I am by taking the easy route. It wasn't easy for me, and it won't be for you. *Life is hard and then you die.* But when you get right down to it, you don't have any other choice but this one: *follow your passions.*

The hardest part is the first step, making the choice to be happy. Living a happy life is a choice, and you are the one to make it. Once you make that choice, everything changes. Your walk, your talk, your smile, your choices, all change because you are happy.

A real Diva knows that when she's happy, the world is a better place.

A real Diva knows that once she finds her joy . . . *it's on!*

I found my joy on the stage. By the end of my freshman year, I'd been invited to compete in the Irene Ryan Scholarship Competition as part of the American College Theater Festival. The Irene Ryan Foundation awards scholarships to outstanding student performers. The late Irene Ryan is best remembered as the feisty Granny in *The Beverly Hillbillies*. Theater departments from around the country nominate their top students to compete, and hundreds of talented actors and actresses practice for months in eligible student productions, hoping to bring top honors back to their colleges and universities.

I was shocked to find out that I had been chosen, and Dr. Bettenbender couldn't have been happier. I was picked based on a performance in a play he had directed, written by a promising student playwright also at Rutgers by the name of Neil Cuthbert. The play was called *The Soft Touch*. Without regard to color, Dr. Bettenbender cast who he felt was the best actress, and the College Festival obviously agreed with him.

He was like a proud father. Freshmen weren't usually chosen to compete, and I'd only been seriously studying theater for a year. The odds were against me, but I didn't even think about that. I just felt honored and figured I'd better get practicing.

To everyone's surprise, I won the regional competition and

was invited to perform in Washington, D.C., at the Kennedy Center for the national title.

I don't remember if I felt nervous or out of place. I might have. But once I stepped onto the stage of the Kennedy Center, I was once again home. I was center stage, where all the worries in the world melted away. In that moment, I was doing what I was born to do. I was sharing the gifts God had given me to a welcoming audience and *I was loving it.*

At the end of my performance the audience exploded with applause. My mother and father were so happy. My grandmother just beamed with the kind of pride words cannot explain. I took my seat with my family and extended family. They had traveled great distances just to see me on that stage. We watched the other students perform and waited anxiously for the results. And then the moment of truth.

Greg Morris, who was in the TV series *Mission: Impossible* and was one of the first black actors to ever star in a hit TV series, was one of the judges. I was so happy just to have been on the same stage as him. I was happy and content. And the biggest surprise of all? *I won.*

They said my name out loud, Sheryl Lee Ralph. I could hardly believe it. I had to pinch myself.

I knew, in that moment, I had found my joy. And when you find your joy, your audience—whoever they may be, from relatives to coworkers to the good Lord above—will all be applauding for you.

*　*　*

Between the Theater Festival scholarship and the scholarship I'd gotten performing in Miss Black Teenage America, I'd made almost $10,000. Any way you look at it, that was a nice chunk of money, and those were figures my father could stand behind.

"Honey," he said with that great voice of his, "you act all you want. You go right on and do it. You act, Sheryl Lee Ralph."

My dad was so happy that I was acting my way through college. Acting was paying for my tuition and he was happy. My mother, however, was another story. It took quite a while—as in *years* and a Tony nomination and paying to rebuild her house in Jamaica—before my mother would agree with him.

Who knows? I might have made an excellent lawyer and maybe even a better doctor.

I, for one, will never know.

And for that I am very, very grateful.

3

A Diva Takes Risks

$\mathscr{S}$tanding in that phone booth at the Los Angeles airport, waiting for my father to call me back with the telephone number of the person who held my future in her hands, seemed to take hours. As soon as I'd said *I love you, Daddy,* and promised him I'd be careful and hung up, I put another dime in the pay phone. His cousin Mabel answered on the first ring.

I would later find out that Mabel always answered on the first ring because she was always near the phone. The phone, I'd soon find out, was near the TV. The TV was near the window. And that, along with the packs of cigarettes she smoked daily, completed her world.

I didn't know it at the time, but Mabel had severe depression. Most people thought Mabel was happy to sit in the window watching the action on the street. The neighbors knew she hadn't been out in a long time, and they knew she wasn't about to go out. But that she might be *afraid* of leaving? Well, that thought never crossed their minds. Back then, we didn't talk about "it." "It" was something you kept to yourself. We didn't know much about mental illness then.

Mabel had a lot on her plate already, and she was about to get something she could never have anticipated. I was on my way, a nineteen-year-old girl with one suitcase and big dreams. Little Sheryl Lee Ralph, bubbling with enthusiasm and ready to take on the whole world.

Mabel had no idea what was about to hit her.

She opened the door with a smile and welcomed me like a sunny day. She had made a space for me in a small back room that was, looking back, the size of one of my *closets* now. And I couldn't have been happier.

I didn't waste time unpacking. I immediately got on the phone and started reaching out to the friends and few contacts I had within the entertainment industry. I checked in with my answering service. Turned out, my acting teacher from the Negro Ensemble Company had been trying to track me down for weeks.

I called him back and learned he was the associate producer on a new Sidney Poitier movie, and a role in the movie was perfect for me! Just like that, before Mabel had a chance to even figure out how long I'd be staying with her, I had gotten called in for an audition with Mr. Sidney Poitier. Me, little Miss Sheryl Lee Ralph, auditioning for *the* Sidney Poitier!

The part was in what would be the last of the Sidney Poitier/Bill Cosby collaborations, and the film would be directed by Sidney Poitier himself. I was thrilled out of my mind. I figured it must be a sign for real . . . less than twenty-four hours in LA, and I had an audition with an Oscar winner. I was exactly where I was meant to be. This first audition might lead to a part, and a part might lead to a Hollywood career. Everything I'd worked for, studied for, and dreamed about was right in front of me, ripe for the picking. And it all started with this one audition.

But there was just one problem . . . I didn't have any way to get there.

Nineteen was too young to rent a car in California, I didn't have a credit card, and a taxi would be way too expensive. Besides, where were the Warner Bros. studios anyway? My only option was to ask Cousin Mabel to drive me.

Well, to say that Mabel freaked out would be putting it lightly. After hours of my begging and soothing, she was still utterly panicked at the idea of driving anyone anywhere. She hadn't been behind a steering wheel in years. In the end, I somehow convinced her. I'd like to believe it was a result of my powers of persuasion, but the truth was simpler. The payoff for driving me to my audition? Cousin Mabel would get to meet Sidney Poitier. For that, Cousin Mabel would do something she hadn't done in years, leave the safety of her TV and window world.

Of course, it wasn't easy. The drive from Mabel's house in LA to the Warner Bros. studio in the Valley should have taken only twenty minutes, twenty-five at the max. Instead, it took Mabel one hour and a whole pack of cigarettes. The whole time, I tried to stay calm and soothing, keeping up a steady stream of positivity. "You're doing it, Mabel. We're almost there, Mabel! See, isn't this fun! Can you believe we're going to meet Mr. Poitier?"

Of course, inside I wasn't feeling as calm. I realized that this was very, very hard for Mabel. She was pushing herself past her comfort zone she'd lived in for so many years.

As the minutes ticked by and Mabel eased her foot off the

gas to light up cigarette after cigarette, I said silent prayers that we'd make it on time.

Then, just like in the movies, there it was, looming before us, seeming to almost glow in the bright California sunshine . . . *Warner Bros. studios. This is it! Hollywood here I am!*

Then I found out about my competition.

Before I'd even stepped in the room to meet with Mr. Poitier, I'd scoped out more information than I knew what to do with. The actresses going up for the part against me? Well, first there was Tamu Blackwell, who'd just come off the movie *Claudine,* starring with one of my inspirations, Diahann Carroll. Of course I'd seen Tamu's performance, and I knew she was a talented actress.

And if that wasn't enough, another actress reading for the role was named Pamela. *Pamela Poitier,* that is. Yes, Mr. Poitier's daughter. Not to mention, also a talented actress. And then there was me.

I thought to myself, *Now, out of these three, who is NOT going to get the role?* The answer was pretty clear to me. In a moment like that, a lot of things are running through your head. And that horrible question couldn't help but rear its ugly head: *What's the point?*

But then I thought about Cousin Mabel. After getting me to the studio, she was so exhausted and drenched with perspiration she wouldn't even come inside to get a glimpse of—let alone meet—her matinee idol. But she had found the strength to leave her house after all those years. Getting there was a miracle in itself; maybe there were more where that one came from.

Not to mention, I had a lot riding on this audition. There

was Cousin Mabel, of course, and my parents, who were probably sick with worry because I had decided to stay in Los Angeles. There was that nagging little voice saying, *What are you doing?!*—which I tried to ignore and push away, but could never quite get rid of it. I'd chosen this route myself, after all.

I had to get myself together. I had to put my best self forward. After all, I could be well on my way to cutting open a cadaver at this point, but I'd taken another direction, and now I had to show the world that I had made the right choice. Yes, I had something to prove. And having something to prove can be a great motivator.

I wanted something more than some great story to tell people about *how I once met Sidney Poitier*. I wanted the part. Sitting there with Tamu and Pamela, I decided that there was no point in being intimidated. I was getting three minutes in a room to audition with an Oscar winner, and I was going to give it my best shot.

Sometimes, in this life, all you'll get is three minutes . . . and I certainly wasn't about to waste a second with second-guessing.

And that is another Diva lesson . . . *a real Diva never backs down against great odds. A real Diva knows that she must take every opportunity and run with it.*

The three minutes themselves are a blur. All I remember clearly is walking into this nice office, and there he was . . . Mr. Sidney Poitier. He immediately reminded me of my father. He was tall and handsome with a warm smile that made me feel comfortable right away. He shook my hand, and I fought the urge to babble on about how much my mother loved him, my grandmother loved him, I loved him. I really fought the urge to tell him about how my dad—as he'd told me many times—missed the opportunity to audition as his understudy in *Raisin in the Sun.*

My dad had to make a serious choice in life: be a father to his daughter and a husband to his wife or chase his own dreams. My dad chose family. In the end, maybe that was why he was so supportive of my choice, and this audition was for both of us.

Everything Mr. Poitier does—from strolling across a room to shake the hand of a young unknown actress to accepting an Academy Award for Best Actor—is done with an innate elegance. There is no way to describe him except to say that he is a true gentleman. From the way he carries himself and speaks to his everyday interactions, Sidney Poitier is a gentleman through and through.

I read the lines I'd practiced and committed to memory. In his presence, I became a star in my head. I read that monologue as if I were an Oscar winner too. I just remember thinking, *That is Sidney Poitier and he's really listening to me.* I was in the same room as *Ebony* magazine royalty, and I was giving that audition everything I had.

When I was done, Mr. Poitier smiled at me again. "I'd like to see you back here next week," he said, his voice businesslike and utterly professional, "for a screen test."

For real? Apparently, two miracles could happen in one day.

In the end, I got the part.

* * *

This was not only my big break, but also the beginning of the most wonderful education a young actress could ever hope to receive. And I had the greatest teacher any wannabe actress could possibly dream of learning from.

Mr. Poitier was extremely kind to me, very much like an uncle. Yes, many men in Hollywood use their power to seduce young girls, but that wasn't Mr. Poitier's style. He was a man of decency with daughters of his own.

Getting that part was one of the greatest gifts I'd ever been given. Sidney Poitier as a director had the utmost respect for his cast.

As for costarring with Bill Cosby? Well, he was an absolute ball of nonstop energy. A wild man with his big old Afro and seventies suits. When he came to the set, everything changed immediately, the mood lightening as he made people laugh. Similar to what it was like having Jamie Foxx on the set of *Moesha* years later.

I often run across Mr. Cosby to this day. We cross paths in Philadelphia, where he went to college and my husband is a state senator. Last time I saw him he had been having trouble with his eyesight. He couldn't even see me, but he recognized my voice. "Sheryl Lee Ralph?" he asked with a smile.

"Yes," I answered.

"Now, Miss Ralph, tell me why that husband of yours isn't with you," he responded with a grin.

Such a flirt.

I didn't spend much time with Mr. Cosby on the set,

though. Most of my scenes were shot in a classroom, which was fitting. The movie itself was a classroom to me, and not all the lessons were easy to learn.

There is a lot of downtime while shooting, and I was a huge reader. My father had put the idea in my head that I should learn something new every day, even if it was just a word. I took that to heart and carried *The People's Almanac* wherever I went. I'll never forget the day I was lost in an especially interesting chapter and didn't hear my name when they called me to take my place on the set.

"Sheryl Lee Ralph," said a deep voice. I jumped. Mr. Poitier stood above me, and everyone was watching. "What are you doing?" he asked me, looking serious.

"I was just . . . um . . . reading a book?"

"Well, I'm just directing a movie. Well, why don't you share with us what has got you so engrossed that you have no idea what's happening on the set?"

"I . . . can't."

He was not having it. "Yes, you can," he responded sternly.

Everyone was watching me, from the production assistants to the key grips. I was so embarrassed that my voice shook.

"Cunnilingus," I said.

I was so deeply embarrassed. I couldn't believe it was happening. I could hear muffled laughter around me. Sidney didn't even flinch. He paid no attention to the chuckling and whispers. Instead, he leaned down and looked at me gravely. "When you're on my set," he said quietly, "pay attention. I'm the director. *I'm the one you should be reading.*"

"I understand."

"Good," he said, standing up. "Then get to work." Before he

turned and strode confidently back to the set, I thought I saw something cross his face. The flicker of an amused smile.

As horrified as I was by the situation, I will be forever grateful for the way he treated me. In that moment, he didn't laugh along with everyone else. Instead, he used that moment to teach me something, and I took his advice to heart. Anything I needed to learn about filmmaking, I could learn right there.

And a Diva knows, there are lessons to be learned everywhere.

This was a true education in the entertainment industry, and I was going to be a star pupil. I had made a mistake and I would learn from it. I watched everything and took it all in. I learned about production, costuming, and lighting. To this day, I know if my lighting is good or not, and I'm not afraid to speak my mind if changes are needed.

That was where I began to learn another Diva lesson . . . a Diva knows to *take an active part in her own life. She doesn't let anyone else take control . . . she takes part in—and helps to form—her own outcome.*

A real Diva has a strong enough ego to learn from her mistakes.

The film, *A Piece of the Action,* is a crime comedy about two thieves—played by Bill Cosby and Sidney Poitier—who are blackmailed into going straight and working at a center for juvenile delinquents. *Really bad* juvies. Desperate to avoid prison time, they take the opportunity.

I played Barbara Hanley, one of the juvies. Remember,

this was 1977, and black America was just beginning to find a voice and it was exploding with a hundred years of pent-up anger. My character brought that anger—especially the young component—to the screen. In a four-minute monologue, I lashed out against the world by lashing out against those nearest me, the teachers who were trying to help me.

I'll never forget filming that scene. There I am, nineteen and in my first film, with an Academy Award winner as my director, playing my first movie role, and what a role it was. Barbara was not at all like me. She was a rough, unhappy girl. She'd just as soon cuss you out as speak to you. But I was going to get to know her and give her life. "Time out! Time out dammit!" began my monologue, and from that moment *it was on*! I just became someone else.

"If we all get jobs, it'll blow your game," I said, my voice seething with anger. "Yeah, your game . . . all you middle-class bougie-ass niggers . . . don't blow smoke up my ass about no f**ckin' job. All us poor, deprived ghetto children . . . Now if it wasn't for niggers like us, y'all wouldn't make shit. Where you live? Not around here, I'll bet you that. . . . My mama didn't raise no fool. What's happen' is I can recognize a poverty pimp when I see one . . . what's happen' is bourgeois bullshit." At one point I even turn to Mr. Durrell, played by Mr. Poitier, and spit, "What y'all niggers make for this jive-ass number you runnin' down on us? Fifteen, twenty thousand?"

I'm often asked how I created that character, where a nice little girl such as me could have found that kind of anger. After seeing the film, even my father was shocked. "I know you're an actress, 'cause I didn't know *who* that girl was," he told me. As an actress, that is a great compliment.

Yes, I was very different from the character Barbara Hanley, but even as a young actress I could understand her. She was a hard-edged child of poverty with a chip on her shoulder. I could understand her pain and ambition. I could feel her fire for life bubbling up from inside me, and I let her voice explode across the screen. Even today, Barbara is still relevant. A great deal has changed, but a lot of young African-American men and women are still burning to learn more and live better, to be understood and appreciated as human beings.

How did I disappear inside that character? It was easy. I knew that girl.

As a child of integration, I always lived straddling the black and white worlds. My parents wanted the best for me, so in the fourth grade they had me take a test for a new school, an exclusive private school. I'd never seen anything like it before.

Public school had huge concrete playgrounds—boys on one side and girls on the other—with a common area in between. But my new school was all green, and there were no boy students at all. I knew I was somewhere special, and I had a feeling that I must be someone special to be allowed inside. What I didn't realize was that many of my classmates and teachers would feel the same way about me, and being special wasn't always a good thing.

That first morning I'd been so excited to put on my new school uniform. There were no uniforms in public school, and this was nothing like the one I wore for Girl Scouts. We had crisp white shirts, blue blazers, knee-length plaid skirts, knee-high socks, and brown, wing-tip shoes. Did I mention the tie? Yes, we had that too. I loved it! I adored the whole ensemble, except the shoes. But as soon as I entered the huge front gates, I realized the uniform wasn't enough to make me fit in.

No one else looked like me. No one else had the same kind of kink in her curls or full lips like mine. I looked at all the girls dressed up and ready to learn on that first day. I thought, *Who'll be my new BFF&E?* My new best friend forever and ever! *Who will I do homework with and tell my secrets to?* As I looked, something became immediately obvious: *I was the only little black girl in a sea of white people.*

The nuns who ran the school stood before us. Not one of them shared my color either.

The school was very organized. We lined up outside in the yard, walking quickly and quietly in single file to our classroom. I will never forget that first day. I took my assigned seat. I even remember where it was, the fourth one in the last row right next to the windows.

I looked outside. I started to cry.

I didn't want to be alone or the only "one" in the entire school. When the nun called on me to answer the first question of the day, I did. That was the beginning. There was no looking back.

My new school life: from 8:30 a.m. to 3:30 in the afternoon, the only black person or Negro I saw was in the girls' room mirror. Making friends wasn't easy, but I did it. These were the kind of friends who found me "entertaining." They wanted to feel my hair and understand how it could stand up on its own. They wanted to touch my skin, as though it would be different from theirs. I quickly discovered that it actually was . . . my skin was tougher.

When those girls called me names, I couldn't let it hurt me.

I had to let it just roll off. I tried to believe what my mother always told me. *Sticks and stones will break my bones but words will never hurt me.* But those words did hurt. They used to say I had *liver lips.* Funny, I bet those same girls pay big money now to have lips like mine. They'd say I was ugly and weird. They used other words they'd probably heard from adults, saying things they probably didn't fully understand themselves. I didn't understand either, but I was learning something: how to keep moving forward and carry on. I was a little girl, but I had to stand strong. I had no other choice.

Then there were the other girls. The things they said were worse. Hate is a strong word, but I hate the N-word. I tried to stand up for myself and waited hopefully for someone to stand up for me. Sometimes a lone voice in the crowd would tell the bullies to leave me alone. It is amazing what one voice can do. There is power in one. I just wish I had heard it more often.

Every Wednesday, the students would take turns going downstairs to the music room for our half-hour lesson. My dad was a talented piano and organ player, and I was expected to play piano as well. My piano teacher was a rigid woman with icy green eyes. She made me uncomfortable. My fingers never seemed to hit the right notes when she was watching. And it didn't help that I hadn't practiced enough.

One day I left my classroom and went straight to my piano lesson. Sister was in a foul mood. My fingers stumbled over the keys and I started over. I guess I started over one too many times, because she walked up behind me and shut the piano lid with a thud, just missing my fingers. "You know," she said, "I don't have to take students like you." Then she just looked at me with that cold gaze.

She sent me back upstairs. I was happy to get away from her, but when I opened the door to my classroom, I saw that my whole class was gone. I was confused. *Where are they? Why did they leave me?* I headed straight over to the principal's office, and they sent me in to see Mother Superior.

I told Mother Superior what had happened. I explained that my class was gone and I didn't know what to do. She acted as though I'd done something wrong. She told me that there were *consequences for lying. Liars were not tolerated at this school.* She walked me back over to my classroom. I tried to keep up with her long, determined strides, watching her black habit billowing out, almost hitting me in the face. *Why would Mother Superior think that I am a liar?*

When Mother Superior opened the door to the classroom, it was empty. I had been left behind. But I was the only "one." *How could they just leave me?* To this day I wonder how and why that had happened.

Mother Superior looked down at me. "Go home," she said.

What had I done to make the piano teacher so angry? Why did my teacher and class leave me? Why did Mother Superior send me home in the middle of the day without even calling my parents? I couldn't figure it all out. *Maybe they're right,* I thought. *Maybe I did something wrong. Maybe I didn't practice enough. Maybe I was a bad girl.*

Years later I know the truth: nothing I could have done would have made a difference. Nothing would have made those women like me, because they didn't like themselves.

At the end of that fourth-grade year, my father was offered the job of assistant principal at a Long Island high school. I was so happy to be leaving. In pursuit of the best for their children, my parents tried to enroll me in another private school.

I made it plain—in no uncertain terms—that was not happening. I told them I was going to public school. They must have heard something convincing in my voice, because they didn't argue.

Everything was better after that. I made lots of friends. These were the kind that have kept in touch and found me years later on Facebook. By middle school, I had found a place for myself in the school hierarchy. I ran for class office, competed in sports, and participated in school clubs. I fit in. Sort of. But what happened in the fourth grade never left me. Those experiences were still there and they still hurt. I just pushed them far away and deep inside. I carried on.

Sometimes a Diva has to leave the hurt behind. To carry it with you only makes it hurt worse.

Everyone, to some degree, has felt like an outsider. We have all had our own version of that piano teacher telling you that you aren't good enough, smart enough, or even the right color. It never feels good. I have learned that when people start telling you how unworthy you are, what they are really saying is they feel deeply unworthy themselves.

As for Barbara, I could play that character because I knew her pain. I understood how she felt having her teacher call her *dumb*. I learned as an actress to call upon my personal memories as inspiration. I had to bring that hurt little girl back to the surface, look her straight in the eyes without flinching and say, "Honey, we are in this together."

I embraced Barbara and I love her still. On the set I felt comfortable and safe enough to let her and all of her hurt and anger live out loud. But what I didn't know at the time was that the world was much more complicated for black actresses beyond Mr. Poitier's safe haven. It wasn't enough just to be talented.

I was picking a road that still needed to be built. This was a time when, as I later told the *New York Times,* black actresses had limited options in terms of casting. Or as I put it, we play an extraordinary range of "welfare mamas and hookers . . . naked or dead."

Young and fresh off *A Piece of the Action,* I didn't know that then. But even if I had, I wouldn't have let it stop me. Like any good Diva, I'd never let anybody tell me what I was or wasn't capable of doing.

That said, nothing was going to come easy. But a good Diva never backs down from her dreams, 'cause she knows her dreams are worth fighting for.

And fight I would.

4

A Diva Fights for Her Dreams

Robert De Niro gave me a reality check that I will never forget. We were on the set of the movie *Mistress,* where I played his strong-willed girlfriend. The scene was in a car, and we were chatting in between takes as the production crew did some lighting adjustments. Robert turned to me. "Sheryl Lee," he said in that real New York accent, "you are really talented. But ya wanna know the truth about this business? You're gonna have to climb that mountain and wave the red flag. Let 'em know you're there 'cause Hollywood *is not* looking for the black girl."

Wow! He just said it. "Hollywood is not looking for the black girl." And the true reality check? This was 1992. If he thought Hollywood was tough on the black girl in the nineties, he should have tried being a black girl in Hollywood in the 1970s.

He was right about it being hard, but here's where he was wrong. Hollywood was *always* looking for "the black girl." I mean, who else was going to play the prostitute?

And I'm not talking about the prostitute with the heart of gold, either. You know "that prostitute" because you've seen her a million times. She sells her body because she has no other choice; she's got to feed her baby/make the rent/cover her tuition 'cause she's a good person underneath it all. She's Julia Roberts in *Pretty Woman*. She's Shirley MacLaine in *Sweet Charity*. She's Nicole Kidman in *Moulin Rouge!*

The black prostitute is a whole different thing. At least that is how I saw it in the late seventies. The black prostitute always got killed first, always had a drug problem. No one had anything nice to say about her, then she was shot and left for dead. And the vast majority of the time, she'd be left dead *and* naked.

When I'd decided to become an actress, these weren't the parts I'd imagined myself playing. I wanted to play parts such as Diahann Carrol's in the television show *Julia*. Julia was a widow raising her son and doing the best she could to be a responsible woman. She was beautiful, smart, and *black*. Well, I *loved* that.

It didn't take much time in Hollywood for me to understand the truth: that show was called *groundbreaking* for a reason. There were rarely parts that good, or realistic, for a black woman. I had dreams of waking up as beautiful as Judy Pace in *Brian's Song*. I wanted to make my mark in movies being *beautifully black*. Or being the first black woman to go where no man has gone before; I wanted to be like Uhura on *Star Trek*.

Coming off *A Piece of the Action*, I was ready for my life in show business to begin. The reviews of my performance were wonderful, and some people said that I should be nominated for something. I couldn't think about that. There wasn't time. I wondered, where was my next movie role? I was young, eager, and God knows I was willing to work hard; I wanted juicy, emotional parts that would challenge me as an actress. I wanted love scenes and death scenes and dialogue full of heartbreak and joy. And I went on many auditions . . . to play *the black prostitute. Or the welfare mama. Or the poor black lady on the couch.*

I just couldn't do it. I just couldn't play those roles.

Once in a while a young actress will ask me how I had the guts to make those choices. Those decisions led to a ten-year wait for my next film role. *Parts are hard to find,* they'd tell me. *I want to work,* they always say. And I understand completely their longing to be working actresses. I wish I could tell you the exact reason I was so choosy about my roles, but it isn't something I can easily explain. I just knew that I had other people to answer to. I never wanted to embarrass my family. Their pride in me was more important than any role or working as an actress at all.

Every actress knows that a "hooker with a heart of gold" is the kind of role that can make you a star. Just ask Shirley MacLaine or Julia Roberts. But it isn't the same for a black actress. Not that I don't love a challenging part. Years later, I would jump at the chance to play the first transgendered character on television in the HBO series *Barbershop.* As an actress, I embrace the opportunity to stretch myself with a role that is both groundbreaking and edgy. Once again, the character was very different from me, but the role was well written. I was playing a human being with emotional depth, wants, real pain, and real dreams.

I loved that part, and it was a risk. The risky roles I didn't want to play? The pimp, the ho, the hooker, and the woe-is-me. Maybe I couldn't put words to it at the time, but I knew in my heart that I wanted more as an actress and a young woman. Being portrayed in that way over and over was detrimental to both the audience and my own well-being.

Even today, I cringe at seeing certain black "housewives" on television. When there are so few parts for African-American women, these shows start to represent all black women. We don't have a balance of multifaceted, positive black female role models coming into our living room weekly. Unfortunately, Michelle Obama does not have a TV show and Oprah ended hers.

Somebody has to be the balance. My grandmother taught me an old saying. For her, it was more than just something to be said, it was something I was meant to live by.

When you walk into a room, the whole race enters with you.

Looking back, I think I had a lot of guts. I wanted to work more than anything else. My worst fear was that I'd be forced to call my daddy and beg for enough money to buy a plane ticket home. But still, despite that fear, I refused over and over to play those kinds of roles.

I don't judge the women who took those parts. Some of them are still working, and they are good actresses, many beautiful and talented. Still, my peers would ask me over and over why I was "being so stubborn." I'd just tell them the truth: *those parts are not for me.* Those parts are not *who I am.*

I was still discovering who I was myself. I was finding my way in the world. But if I ever—even just for a moment— considered the possibility of playing a hooker (dead or alive),

I'd just think about my mom and dad sitting proudly in front of the TV to watch my television debut as a *dead, black, naked whore*. I didn't ever want to play a part that my parents wouldn't be proud of seeing me in. I wanted my grandmother and the folks at church to be proud of me too. Worse than failing as an actress was the overwhelming fear that I'd disgrace my family, and their approval meant the world to me.

Not to mention my grandmother's saying stayed with me. I would not do anything I felt would disgrace my race either.

I blame (and thank) my parents for this stubbornness. They kept me grounded enough to say what I *would* and *wouldn't do*. At that time, it was mostly what I *wouldn't do,* and it wasn't easy, all those disappointments. Finally getting called in to read by that big casting director, then handed a page of script with two lines of caricatured, ghetto-fied dialogue that was written by some old white guy who would never dream of going within ten miles of a *real* ghetto. And this old white guy was going to tell me how to *be* black? How to *sound* black?

The world was changing. Black people were finding their voices. There was anger and outrage. There was the cry for equality and change.

Unfortunately, television isn't the real world, and it was changing at a much slower rate. Casting agents were confused as to what to do with me. One told me—and the words haunted me for years—*that I was obviously talented and beautiful, but what was he going to do with a beautiful, talented black girl? Put me in a movie opposite Tom Cruise? Do we kiss? Who goes to see THAT movie?*

Even now, some find an interracial kiss on-screen unnerving. Back then, the idea was practically laughable. No network would dare put that out there for America to see; at the very least, there would be a huge outcry. More likely, there would be protests.

So, yes, my options were limited. Only a handful of black television shows were around, and those few walked a fine line between reality and pure stereotype. And those shows that Hollywood created to show their version of the "true, authentic black American experience"? Well, they were overwhelmingly created, produced, written, and directed by *white* people. The black people? We had to be satisfied playing "the black people."

As Redd Foxx revealed later, at one point he actually walked away from his starring role on the hit show *Sanford and Son* because of a complete lack of black directors and writers. *The white producers,* he believed and publicly stated, *not only didn't know about black culture, but they didn't care to find out.*

And Mr. Foxx might just have been right.

There's one audition I'll never forget. I was reading for *Sanford,* the spin-off of *Sanford and Son.* I got to read for a real bigwig, Bud Yorkin. He was one of the creators, and the kind of guy who could snap his fingers and make a struggling young actress into a star.

I was excited and nervous. This was my big chance! This was one of the few network TV pilots with a black cast and a young female lead. And I'd been called in to read for that plum role, and she *was not* a prostitute. After a lack of quality roles for young black women, this was the opportunity I'd been praying for.

I got lots of sleep the night before. The next morning I ate a healthy breakfast, took extra care in picking my outfit and doing my vocal warm-ups.

When I got in that room with Mr. Yorkin, my nervousness faded away. Just as in that moment with Mr. Poitier, I knew I had three minutes, and I was going to give it my best shot. Mr. Yorkin, sitting with his assistant, nodded to me. I took a deep breath.

Then I read my lines. I read my little heart out.

I finished, flushed with happiness. I'd done a good job and I knew it. I looked at Mr. Yorkin. I can only imagine my young face, glowing and hopeful, just waiting for that tiny little word that would change everything. That yes that would launch my career.

"Here's the thing," he said. "You just aren't right for this part. To be completely honest with you . . . well, you just *aren't black enough.*"

I felt my whole body go numb. Did he just tell me I *wasn't black enough?* He kept talking, probably telling me exactly *how black enough he believed I wasn't,* but I don't remember a word he said. I just looked down at my clasped, *obviously black* hands. They were shaking.

I don't remember if I said good-bye, but I know I left with my chin held high. If I was going to cry, I'd do it far away from that audition room. No one was going to break me. At least, not in public.

I'd been black enough to be called in for numerous parts playing *black prostitutes,* but I wasn't black enough to play *a black woman with education and drive?* What did that even mean? My ancestors had been African slaves, and I *wasn't black enough?* This wasn't like telling an actress she needed to lose twenty pounds or dye her hair a different color or even get a nose job. This man was saying that who I am and the identity I was born with *was not good enough.*

For a moment, I considered quitting. Everything. I thought about going home to my parents and having them hold my hands and tell me everything would be fine and that I'd done my best.

Then my mother would bring up med school . . . or where I could find a good doctor to marry.

But one thing about me—my gift and my burden—is that I'm not a quitter. And sometimes the word *no* just makes you want it more. Somehow, deep inside, I knew it would be okay, the tide would turn and somebody would do right by me. And something else I knew: *that man wouldn't know a black person if he or she was standing right in front of him.*

That was a hard-learned Diva life lesson: *a no today can be a yes tomorrow.* And there would be many other ones of a similar nature. If I chose to stay in Hollywood, that kind of rejection was bound to happen again. Again and again. But what do you do, my lovely Divas-in-training, when faced with a risk? Do you let go of those dreams? Do you, as that visionary man Langston Hughes once wrote, *let them dry up like a raisin in the sun?*

Well, I think we both know the answer to that. H to the NO!

Because here is the truth: *life is a risk.* Life is a risk when the light turns red and you cross the street thinking everyone is going to stop. What if someone doesn't? Life is a risk when you take out a credit card and buy something on the Internet. What if someone takes your name and steals your identity?

Life is a risk when you get married and say those vows; will that other person feel the exact same way until death do you part?

The answer is this: *I have no idea.* Life can be hard, and there are no set answers, but what is the alternative? Death is, and that isn't much of an alternative. Life is a risk, and life is for the living. So go after what you want. And when people tell you that you are crazy, or it will never happen, or that you're *not black enough or white ain't right or you're too fat or too thin or too young or too old or too smart or just not dumb enough?* Well, who said *they* know everything . . . or anything at all? *They* are just people like you and me.

And you can never be sure . . . you might just see them, years later. And they might just look at you, their eyes full of new understanding, and say *they made a mistake.* Or, as Mr. Yorkin put it when I ran into him at a Hollywood function decades later, "Not casting you in that show was a real mistake. I don't know what I was thinking. I'm sorry. You are a wonderful actress, Sheryl Lee Ralph."

I smiled and said, "Thank you." I could see in his eyes . . . he knew the pain he had caused me, and there was no point in holding a grudge. Besides, I am a firm believer in letting bygones be, well, *gone.* Except, of course, when you're writing a book for your fellow Divas and *want to make a point.*

Anyway, I'm sure we were both thinking the same thing, how that little show, the one I hadn't been *black enough* for, was so awful that NBC pulled it from the airwaves after only four episodes.

And that is how the cookie crumbles.

5

A Diva Doesn't Quit

didn't leave Hollywood. If anything, that *Sanford* experience made me push ahead even harder. *Yes, Mr. De Niro, I waved that red flag.* And I kept waving. In fact, I'm still waving it.

I went back to pounding the pavement, but now with a renewed energy. Showbiz is full of rejection, you will get a hundred noes to that one important yes. But I grew stronger and more confident, and those *no* moments seemed less and less important. I just had to keep studying, keep my look and outlook fresh. What kept me going was the knowledge that I was born to perform, and no other life path would make me as happy. Keeping that knowledge close to my heart put everything—even the rejection—in perspective.

Remember, Diva-in-training, people who have made it to great heights struck out on their own and took chances. *It wasn't always easy for them, and it won't always be easy for you. But it will be worth the climb.*

*   *   *

I didn't know it then, but I was *already* waving that red flag. I stuck it out, taking classes, praying the way my mother had taught me and keeping the faith. Then, one day, the tide turned. I got one part. The part wasn't huge, but I was blown away. I'd be playing George Jefferson's secretary on the hit TV sitcom *The Jeffersons*. In an odd way, it seemed fated.

Sherman Hemsley, who played George Jefferson, was someone I'd looked up to for years. In high school I had the chance to see him in the Broadway musical *Purlie*. I loved that musical. Sherman and his costar Melba Moore were amazing. I remember sitting in the audience and being mesmerized. I could see myself onstage one day. I'd gotten the chance to meet Sherman briefly backstage, and he'd been so nice to me. I was just a high school kid, and his warmth had a huge effect on me. And now, all these years later, I had my first real part on a show in which he was starring!

George Jefferson was an over-the-top character, while Sherman himself always seemed shy and unassuming. On *The Jeffersons* set, I told him how much he inspired me. He seemed to know how important this first real job was to me, because he went out of his way to be kind and supportive.

Those early kindnesses never leave you. More than a decade after I met him on *The Jeffersons,* I was on *Designing Women*. When they needed someone to play my father, I suggested that Sherman be cast. The producers agreed with me, and it was extraordinary to have Sherman on the set of a TV show with me after all those years had passed.

We hadn't seen each other in a long time, and we had a lot of catching up to do. I reminded him how he'd inspired me as a high school student when I saw him on Broadway. I thanked him for treating me like an equal on *The Jeffersons,* especially since he was the lead, and stars can be notoriously nasty to the guest stars. I was just a young actress in her first real TV part. It would have been just as easy for him to ignore me, and instead he'd encouraged me. For all that, I told him I was forever grateful.

Sherman told me he had followed my career and was especially thrilled that, just like him, I'd gone to Broadway. He told me how proud it made him to see that I'd grown into a strong woman with a thriving career.

We couldn't stop smiling.

In our last scene together on *Designing Women,* all those years of struggles and triumph were right there with us. We'd both worked hard for our careers, and we were still going strong. We stood there, on the set of that hit show, and Sherman looked at me and said his final line to me: "I just love you so much." Instantly, we both burst into tears. The whole audience erupted with a spontaneous "Awwww," but that moment didn't require *acting* from either of us. We shared a legacy.

The Jeffersons role led to more auditions, which led to a guest-starring role that led to another, and before I knew it, that nineteen-year-old girl who'd told her dad *right now I have to be here* from a telephone at the Los Angeles airport . . . well, that girl was a little older and a little wiser and she had an actual, undeniable *television acting career.* And she'd done it without playing any parts that would have embarrassed her family or, more important, herself.

Success can and does happen, and it can happen without compromising yourself. It might be harder to get there, but in the end you'll be able to live with the decisions you made. And here are the keys: *never give up and know just how far you'll go to make it or to get that job.*

A Diva knows her bottom line!

If you are faced with a decision you are unsure about or feel might compromise you, imagine some people important to you and picture their faces. How will they feel if you do this? I never played a part that would embarrass my family, and I never slept with someone for a part. If you sleep with someone for a part, you know what you'll get? *Laid.*

Most of the time, I wouldn't let it get to the casting-couch point. Of course, I had a few unavoidable moments when I was propositioned by someone who claimed he could help my career if I just slept with him, took that trip to Vegas, did a li'l something else. But I knew my bottom line, I knew how far I'd go. I'd just say this: *I don't do that.*

Cast me first, and then maybe I'll sleep with you. But only if I really want to.

What it comes down to is this: *I am not a gambling woman.* Not with my career, not with my money, and certainly not with my body. I know that sleeping with someone in the hope that the person will cast you is a *bad bet.* And I don't like to lose money, let alone myself.

A Diva-lesson: giving up your cookies won't get you anything but eaten.

* * *

As tough as the climb was then—and continues to be now—eventually my talent, training, and drive were a winning combination. Only a handful of shows had all-black casts, and somehow I found my way on enough of them to make a difference for my life and my career. True, these shows weren't perfect in their depictions of real black people, but they gave African-American audiences the chance to see characters of their own color with actual story lines. In that way, these shows were ahead of their time, and I'm proud to have been a part of them.

To this day, people come up to me because they remember seeing me in *Good Times,* when I played J.J.'s uppity girlfriend who couldn't go bowling because "It'll be murder on my lip gloss!" They remember my being on *The Jeffersons* and want to know what went on behind the scenes.

The truth about those shows, those forerunners in black entertainment that paved the way for the Cosbys, Ravens, and Brandys of today, is that there were so few shows and opportunities for black actors, we felt lucky to be working at all. This was before there were entire lineups of shows—let alone networks—featuring brothers, sisters, and others.

When people ask about those early shows, I know they want the juicy gossip on catfights and chaos. Well, I don't have those stories to tell. At least not from that time in my career. Of course, things are always changing, and future television sets would offer more drama . . . but more on *Moesha* later.

When I first started out in the business, I felt a sense of community. I'll never forget my time on *The Jeffersons.* That was a show the likes of which America had never before seen. If you think about it today, it doesn't sound that edgy: a black couple who become successful and "move on up" to a wealthier lifestyle with a deluxe condo on the East Side and that famous theme song: "Fish don't fry in the kitchen"! And even more controversial than black people living that upper-class lifestyle, the interracial couple that lived downstairs.

Pretty tame stuff by today's standards. But in the late seventies, Norman Lear was pushing the envelope, and some people found the show absolutely shocking. Perhaps the actors weren't always aware that what they were doing was so ahead of the times, but they knew they were doing something special and watched out for each other.

Roxie Roker, who played Helen Willis, was the black part of the interracial couple on *The Jeffersons*. She must have understood the interracial prejudice well: in real life, her husband was white, pretty brave in that time, and even to some extent in this day. Roxie was an elegant woman with a kind heart. I was just starting out, and she was giving and helpful. She was simply wonderful, giving me advice in her dressing room, inviting me over to her home for Thanksgiving because she knew I'd be lonely with my family across the country.

Her husband, Sy, was a nice man, and, lord, he *loved him* some Roxie. And I'll never forget their son, a bright, forward-thinking teenager with his modern-cut 'fro and argyle vest, always hanging around the set and taking everything in. Roxie was so proud of him. "My son, Lenny," she'd tell me, "he's going to be a great artist. Just you wait."

In the end, little Lenny Kravitz did just fine for himself.

Whenever I see him, a grown man with a beautiful child of his own, all those memories flood back. I remember him on the set saying, always with respect and manners, "Ms. Ralph, when are you going to let me write a song for you?" Maybe someday he will.

Roxie passed away of breast cancer when she was still young and vibrant. But she touched my life in a special way, and I will never forget her glowing spirit. She grew ill and lost her hair, but never lost her warmth and dignity. She kept her door open to others as long as she could. Her death was a great loss.

Things picked up quickly after I got that first part on *The Jeffersons*. The eighties had just begun, and everything I'd worked for was beginning to pay off. I had a real television career, and there were new opportunities every day. I was a working actress and determined to keep working. I'd fought hard for my career, and I was enjoying every moment of success because I'd earned it.

Then, just like that, I got a call asking me to give up everything. Did I want to go to New York and audition for a musical? If I got the part, I'd have to leave behind what I'd worked so hard for in Hollywood. Yes, theater was my first love. Since that first audition for Dr. Bettenbender, I'd known that the stage was where I felt most alive. But still, did I want to leave the glamour and huge audience of television? Was I willing to take a big pay cut and work myself to the bone doing eight shows a week after how hard I'd worked to establish a career in Hollywood?

If you know me at all by now, the answer is obvious . . . *of course I did.*

6

A Diva Embraces the Chaos

$\mathcal{S}$ome musicals go down in history for their innovation and acclaim. Then there are the ones that go down in history for a completely different reason: they were *notorious flops*. *Reggae* was in the second category.

Reggae was to be producer Michael Butler's black version of his smash Broadway hit, *Hair*. Nothing heavy-handed . . . just peace, love, and ganja. There were elaborate, colorful costumes, sexy Rude Boys in leather, Jamaican Rastafarians celebrating Judaism complete with beautifully choreographed happy, huge, trippy musical numbers. But what was the musical about? Well, the plot of all great musicals and movies is the same: boy meets girl, boy loses girl, boy gets girl again. In this musical the girl was Faith, a popular Jamaican singer who returns home to find herself. While there, she also finds her lost love, Esau (played by Philip Michael Thomas of *Miami Vice* fame), who has become a ganja farmer/low-key drug dealer.

With a production that included names such as Michael Butler and Melvin Van Peebles, *Reggae* also had the wonderful Michael Kamen as musical director. Michael blessed me with a wonderful song, "Everything That Touches You." He was a lovely man and a great talent.

Stellar Jamaican artists were on the production team as well, including Stafford Harrison, Kendrew Lascelles, Ras Karbi, Max Romeo, and Jackie Mittoo.

With that kind of talent, it should have been a hit.

Well, you can't win them all.

This was the kind of show Broadway had never before seen, and people wouldn't see it for long. The show closed almost as fast as it opened. *Reggae* opened on March 27, 1980, and closed April 13, for a total of twenty-one performances.

Of course, when I got the call to audition for *Reggae,* I didn't know all this. All I knew was that this Broadway show was in previews and opened in ten days, and they needed a star leading lady *now,* as the beauty queen playing Faith had been fired. The word around the show was she'd been hired for her looks and not her acting abilities. A classic Broadway tale, but now that the show was about to open, there was one big problem. It was obvious she couldn't act *to save her life or the show.* A friend of mine and friend to this day, Jeffrey Anderson-Gunter, was in the company and heard about the situation and called me.

I had just been fired from director/producer Stuart Ostrow's musical *Swing!* Quick summary: *Midsummer Night's Dream* plays out around a baseball game with four downtown white kids and four uptown black kids, filled out with a jazzy score. Hit or flop? *Flop!* Ostrow fired all four of the black actors in the cast because, as he put it, we "no longer fit stylistically in the show." They left us on the road in Baltimore and went on to open at the Kennedy Center, where they quickly closed. Bobby LuPone and Janet Eilber (who went on to lead the Martha Graham Dance Company) couldn't save that show.

I was devastated. It hadn't been an easy production from day one, and I didn't understand why they just left us. I know the show must and will go on, but, gee! I cried till my nose hurt and my eyes turned red as rubies. And then Jeffrey called telling me to stop the tears and get on the first train smoking back to New York. He told me that he knew Michael Butler would hire me if he saw me. The next morning I was back in Manhattan standing at the stage door of the Biltmore Theatre with my suitcase in hand.

One door closes and a stage door opens!

I'd always dreamed of being on Broadway. There is nothing like the excitement of performing for a live audience, as anything could happen. And in the case of a musical such as *Reggae,* it would. Once again, I had no idea what was in store, but it didn't matter. This was a chance, and I was going to dive in headfirst as any true Diva would.

Michael Butler, the hippie millionaire producer, was big-time. He'd been the visionary who took a little off-Broadway hippie musical with a crazy little script and turned it into the hugely successful Broadway musical *Hair. Reggae,* originally titled *Irie,* was meant to be the successful follow-up with the same unique hippie-inspired aesthetic with reggae music thrown in for flavor. There were hopes of a musical that would be revolutionary.

When I arrived at the Biltmore Theatre stage door, the entire cast was milling around, praying that the show would go on. You could feel the tension in the air. After all, it was ten days until the opening, and no leading lady. After one preview it was obvious that the Beauty Queen was not a Broadway Baby. My friend Jeffrey found me, his face lighting up like that of a thirsty man who'd seen a waterfall in the Sahara. He took me by the hand to meet Michael Butler. Michael Butler watched from the audience, his face a stone mask.

I immediately introduced myself. I used the Jamaican accent I'd learned from my mother. Michael Butler perked up. He asked musical director Michael Kamen to teach me "Everything That Touches You."

I began to sing, but Michael Butler didn't even let me finish. I was hired on the spot.

Just like Dorothy, I had been lifted into a tornado, and the next week was an exciting blur. I barely had time to call friends and family. Within hours of the audition, I was being given a crash course in Broadway while trying to remember the choreography and blocking for a show that opened in ten days. There wasn't time for me to be nervous, let alone fully take in that I was opening as *the lead in a Broadway show*.

Two days later, I was onstage for the critics' preview. I was still holding a script in my hand.

The whole experience was an excitingly choreographed chaos. Working onstage with a cast is a team effort and requires a sense of trust. We trust that each other knows his or her lines and gives you your cues. The lighting and sound people depend on you to move to the right place at the right time so they know their cues as well. A whole show should tick like a tightly wound watch. Almost immediately, the cast of *Reggae* became my new family.

Calvin Lockhart, who had starred in many blaxploitation

films, was a black version of Michelangelo's *David*. So beautiful with skin like shiny ebony marble. There was the rising
Jamaican reggae singer and one of the show's composers, Ras
Karbi. In other words, there was plenty of male eye candy,
including Obba Babatundé, a triple-threat performer who'd
just returned from touring with Liza Minnelli. Obba was an
amazing natural dancing man with the kind of innate confidence that lit up a stage. He was a passionate actor who would
become an important part of my young life. That relationship
would lead to his being fired from another, more famous musical, but I knew nothing of *Dreamgirls* yet.

Reggae was chock-full of talent: dancers Kiki Shepard,
Brenda Braxton, and Ralph Glenmore; singer Louise Robinson;
Jamaican actors and my close friends Jeffrey and Tommie Pin-
nock. But all that talent wasn't enough to keep the show afloat.

We opened the day of the transit strike and closed around
the time of the garbage strike. It seemed those gray-haired
Broadway matinee audiences didn't quite like or understand
the concept of black, dreadlocked, Rastafarian, Jamaican Jews
smoking marijuana and dancing with the Star of David to a
reggae sound track.

To tell you the truth, *I* didn't understand some of the show
myself.

So my Broadway career seemed as though it would end just
as quickly as it started. Or so I thought. But the world is funny
that way, my Diva friends. Sometimes one stage door has to
close for another to open real wide!

* * *

Tom Eyen, the genius writer, was in the audience on one of those empty matinee days. Imagine a theater that held a thousand people, with only sixteen people in the audience. That's enough to break an actor's heart and spirit. But after that particular matinee, Tom Eyen came backstage.

Tom Eyen had written for Bette Midler when she was entertaining in the infamous New York bathhouses. He was a smart, edgy writer and didn't mind pushing the envelope of his work to the artistic edge. Maybe he could see the future of *Reggae* before the rest of us, because he was more interested in telling me about a new project he was working on and suggested that I audition. "I might have your next show," he told me. "It doesn't have a name yet but it's a hit."

How could I know that—because of that one little backstage conversation—my life was about to change forever? I was only twenty-three. A month earlier I'd been fired from a big flop of a show. Now here I was in New York in another show destined to flop, and this man says he might have my next part in a show without a name and it's gonna be a hit. Go figure. Every day brought something new and unexpected, but I was doing what I loved, and in that uncertainty was a great sense of excitement.

When I look back at the young girl I was, giddy with the energy and possibility the future held, I wish I could take her hand. "Take a deep breath," I'd tell her. "And get ready for the ride of your life."

* * *

Looking back, my Diva sisters, the next few years would give me some of the highest—and lowest—moments in my life. There would be confusion and anger, elation and undeniable joy.

And now, as I reflect on everything, well, this Diva wouldn't take a moment of it back.

That little show Tom Eyen was developing for Nell Carter wouldn't stay unnamed for long. After a long workshop process with Joseph Papp—who tagged it Project 9—it would go into an even longer workshop process with Michael Bennett before it became *Dreamgirls*.

And *Dreamgirls* really would be revolutionary. Not to mention, for all of us involved, a revelation.

7

A Diva Gets Her Dream

When *Reggae* closed, I was disappointed. It was cold outside and I was hit with the cold reality that the show was over when that closing notice went up. But now that I'd had a taste of Broadway, I knew I wanted more. That said, even with a Broadway show under my belt and a personal invitation to audition for Tom Eyen's new *unnamed, gonna-be-a-hit musical,* I was a mess of nerves in the waiting room of the audition.

The room was packed with black women, many of whom could not just sing, but *sang!* You could see the anticipation on their faces as each one waited for her own three minutes in the room. Musicals with black leads rarely graced Broadway. That might be why they call it the Great White Way. There were some—shows such as *The Wiz, Purlie,* and *Eubie!*—but there never seemed to be enough opportunities, especially for young black actresses.

No one wanted to screw up this opportunity to play something other than the sexy hottentot, the wise-mammy character with a short solo in the second act, or Chorus Girl #4 (black).

I found a place to sit. I waited, and it felt like hours before a man with a clipboard called my name.

The moment I entered the room and Tom Eyen smiled at me, my whole body relaxed. He sat behind a long table with a few other men who lacked his enthusiasm and looked either exhausted or bored.

"Sheryl Lee!" he said, exhaling with great drama. "Are you ready to sing for us, darling?"

"Yes, I am. Thank you." Those manners my mother had drilled into me were still there.

Before I could open my mouth to sing my prepared audition song, he cut me off. "Sing us some gospel. The first thing that comes into your head."

I should have known. I'd overheard the ladies in the waiting room talking about the show. It was still a mystery to us all, but some had heard rumors of a gospel-inspired script. My mind went blank. Being a quietly raised Episcopalian, gospel was not my forte. I only visited the Baptist church once a month or so because my dad was the minister of music.

So I just opened my mouth and sang the first thing that came into my head—a pure, simple "Ave Maria."

When I finished, the room was silent. *I really messed this one up,* I thought to myself. *Why didn't I prepare better? But how could I?*

I saw one of the men behind the table roll his eyes. He leaned back with a sigh. I could tell they'd had a long day.

"Thank you, Sheryl Lee," said Tom.

"You're welcome!" I left the room. I took my seat back in the waiting room, where we'd been asked to stay until we were dismissed. *He asked for gospel,* I chastised myself, *and I gave him "Ave Maria"!? I should leave and go home right now. I should get on the plane and head right back to Hollywood. I had a nice run of it in New York. I gave it my best chance. I only hope they haven't forgotten about me in California.*

I stayed anyway. Of course I did.

The day passed in a fog. Periodically, the man with the clipboard would call names. "Thank you for coming," he'd say, and women would hold back tears or mutter angrily to themselves as they gathered their belongings. Some shot straight for the elevator in a huff.

The day felt like an eternity, as different combinations of girls were brought in and others were asked to leave. It was like an early *American Idol.* They didn't call me in to sing again, and I had no idea why they'd kept me hanging around. *Maybe it was a mistake,* I thought. I waited for something to happen. And waited.

Hours later, something finally did.

"Loretta Devine, Ramona Brooks . . . and Sheryl Lee Ralph," said the man. I reached down for my bag. "Could you come in? And the rest of you may leave. Thank you for your time."

I had no idea in that moment how much my life was about to change. As he said those three words as familiar to me as my own heartbeat—*Sheryl Lee Ralph*—I was about to make the transition from struggling young actress Sheryl Lee to Sheryl Lee, Broadway Star.

In the future I'd be called many names besides Sheryl Lee. I'd be called Diva, a role model, and a rebel. Though I had no idea at the moment, the next few years would bring the adoration of many and the fear of others. There would be admiration toward me that would make me blush, and criticism so harsh I'd grit my teeth. To some I'd represent the breaking down of barriers and the opening of doors for other young women who looked like me. To others, no matter the success I'd have, I'd never go beyond being a black actress in a white industry. As one agent told me, "Don't be like that Diana Ross. Remember *your place*."

Of course, in that moment I had no idea all the things I would become, or all the experiences yet to come. And I'm glad I didn't. The next stage of my life would be one of the roughest and most exciting journeys I could possibly imagine. In so many ways, I was still a girl, but I don't think you could ever be ready for the kind of events that would follow, no matter how young or old you were.

The words rang in my head: ". . . and Sheryl Lee Ralph."

This was just the beginning.

8

A Diva Struggles

*F*ew people believed in Project 9. To many, a show based around three young girls, three *black girls* at that . . . well, nothing like that had ever before been done. *This musical,* as Tom Eyen saw it, would tell the story of a trio of young black singers from Chicago with big voices and even bigger dreams. In fact, they'd be called The Dreams, and the musical would follow their rise to international stardom.

Nothing was set in stone. In those early stages, the show was merely a concept, and a concept strange enough to turn off the majority of mainstream Broadway backers. *What kind of audience would Project 9 bring?* they'd ask. This wasn't standard Broadway stuff. Unlike "classic Americana" musicals such as *Oklahoma!* there weren't any dancing cowboys or pretty blond, milkmaid-looking white girls singing about the dream man they hoped would come and sweep them off their feet. Project 9 wasn't the kind of material thought to pull in a crowd. And though it was only said in private conversations, few believed a cast led by black women would bring in a mainstream audience.

Nothing like Project 9 had been done before. A cast of women characters—and strong black women characters at

that—was truly ahead of the times. One of the few musicals
with a somewhat ethnic cast to receive widespread fame, *West
Side Story,* had even cast a white woman to play Maria, the
Puerto Rican lead. There was no disguising the black faces
that made up the future cast of Project 9, that is, if anyone
believed in the show enough to give it a chance.

But Tom Eyen never gave up.

The first series of rehearsals for Project 9—known to some
as a workshop—were financed by theater legend Joseph Papp.
A workshop is where a musical is given creative space to grow
and take shape. The cast is important to this process, and
we were deeply connected to the making of the show, often
helping to write and arrange songs, helping write the show
itself by improvising dialogue.

Tom Eyen intended the project to be a star vehicle for Nell
Carter, who had just won a Tony for her work in *Ain't Misbe-
havin'.* It is hard to imagine those early days now that Project
9, turned *Dreamgirls,* has gone on to become legendary, but
there was just the circle of us sitting around a table. We spent
the rehearsals practicing early variations of the songs and
helped to create the story of the Dreams. *Dreamgirls* in that
time was still finding a voice, and it was much different from
the final voice of the show the world knows today. It was hard
work creating our page in music theater history.

I was just thrilled to be there. I could hardly believe my
luck. I pinched myself every day to make sure it was really
happening. There I was at a table with some of the most gifted
women I'd ever seen, and we were working together to create
this story.

Of course, it would be a long road to get there.

I was in awe of Nell Carter. She was a big woman with an even larger talent who described herself as a *black, bisexual, Jewish singin' lady.* At times a prickly personality, Nell had demons she was fighting.

I was given the unofficial job of "checking on" Nell during rehearsals. It never crossed my mind to say no. I would probably have picked up everyone's laundry if they'd asked me.

Nell's behavior was at times erratic and increasingly more unpredictable. I'll never forget one day when we were workshopping a song. She stood in the center of the room, belting out the lyrics in that huge, marvelous voice. Then, just like that, she stopped midnote and headed out the door.

Tom raised his eyebrows at me as if to say, *Follow her.* So I did. I headed down the hall, wondering where she could have gone. That's when I heard the noises—strange moaning from the bathroom. I felt my heart begin to race. It sounded as if she were dying.

The bathroom door was slightly ajar. "Nell?" I said. "Are you okay?" There was more moaning. My head was spinning. *What if she's having a heart attack? What if she's dying?* I'd be responsible for the death of one of America's greatest talents, and the show hadn't even opened yet. *Me and the drama!*

My hand shaking, I pushed the door open. I felt my breath catch in my throat. There she was, that gifted, larger-than-life woman filling up that tiny space as she hunched over the toilet bowl, sobbing and heaving. I was scared. "Nell?" She didn't seem to know I was there. "Nell?" I said again, even louder.

Nell turned around to look at me. Her eyes were bright red and she was covered in vomit. I'll never forget the look on her face. It was more of a glare, as if she could see straight through me. As if to say, *You know absolutely nothing about the real world, little girl.*

Watching her, I knew she was right. She heaved herself up and came at me. "Stay away from the hard stuff," she growled, and pushed me out of the bathroom.

I had a lot to learn.

Soon after, Nell left the workshop. She was going to Hollywood, to star in a new TV sitcom called *Gimme a Break,* where she would play the wisecracking maid. Part of me felt relieved. That look on her face—and her admonition to stay away from the hard stuff—had scared me. That was the first time I'd seen the reality of drug addiction, and it wouldn't be the last. I knew that my body and voice were my instruments. They were God's gift to me, and I wasn't going to destroy them with any stuff, especially this mysterious "hard stuff." In some ways, seeing Nell like that was good for me, though her expression would continue to haunt me for decades.

That is a Diva lesson you've heard before, but let me say it again. *Don't do anything that will cause you to lose yourself, because the parts you lose today you might need tomorrow. And more often than not, they are the most beautiful parts of you.*

As soon as Nell left the show, Joseph Papp did too. We had lost the backing of the Public Theater. Without Nell, the Tony Award–winning star, his hope of making a hard-sell show into a Broadway hit would be tough. He must have figured there was a much easier sell out there. Project 9 was shelved.

Tom Eyen was upset, but he believed in Project 9, and Tom

was no quitter. He hit the streets again, trying to find a partner who saw the same potential in this little "dream" project that he did.

I took off on another tour of duty with the armed forces to see the other side of the world and sing my heart out for our troops.

Eventually, Tom found a potential partner in Michael Bennett. Bennett was a superstar, fresh off directing and choreographing the smash hit *A Chorus Line*. Michael knew how to really workshop a show, having done it with *A Chorus Line* to great success.

Bennett agreed to finance a second workshop of Project 9. Once he was on board, the project really picked up steam. The first time I met Michael, he seemed nice enough, if a bit intense.

If I had only known then what I know now.

The creation of *A Chorus Line* by Michael Bennett is the stuff of Broadway legends, not to mention Broadway cautionary tales. *A Chorus Line* went on to become one of the most successful shows in Broadway history, with revival after revival for decades to come.

At the heart of the musical were a series of recordings made in 1974. The participants were mostly unknown actors, struggling hopefuls who barely made ends meet. They shared their real-life stories, allowing Michael Bennett to tape-record them.

These young actors signed contracts—in exchange for a

single dollar, they gave away all rights to these interviews. Most likely, many of these struggling performers held secret hopes that they'd be cast in this new show by this young, hot director interviewing them.

Many of their stories went word for word into the final book for *A Chorus Line*. Talented actors would portray their personal stories for decades to come, touching the hearts of rapt audiences around the world.

These young actors could not know any of this at the time. They were young, talented men and women fighting for their seemingly impossible dream . . . to *make it*. Just like the famous refrain from the show: "God, I hope I get it! I hope I get it!"

The history of these men and women—and how they have been compensated for their part in creating the show—has been shrouded in much mystery and legal silencing. Of these thirty-seven men and women, eight went on to star in the show when it opened on Broadway. Unfortunately, the others were left behind. *A Chorus Line* went on to earn millions, and there have been countless lawsuits over fair compensation for the real people behind the show's characters.

The majority of these thirty-seven kids were Broadway "gypsies" who survived show to show. They lived packed into tiny apartments and pounded the pavement from audition to audition. They waited, hopeless and breathless, for their big break.

The interviews taped by Michael Bennett were of their own heartache, drama, hopes, and triumphs.

Michael Bennett was a brilliant man, able to take these raw stories and turn them into theater.

Much has been written about the process of making *A Chorus Line* and the subsequent lawsuits. What is publicly known is that many of these original interviewees have been somewhat compensated, though it took decades of struggling to reach a settlement.

These were kids who, like so many others, willingly gave up stability to pursue the uncertainty of a Broadway future. Above all, they waited for their big break. Their moment to shine center stage.

In so many ways, I was one of them.

Not much has been said about the creation of *Dreamgirls,* which evolved through a process that was both different from and similar to that of *A Chorus Line.*

Among the differences: fewer of us were involved in the creation of *Dreamgirls.* Among the similarities: we were very much a part of bringing these characters, and their stories, to life. And, yes, we signed the same kind of contract those *A Chorus Line* gypsies had signed.

I, Sheryl Lee Ralph, sign away my contribution to the creation of Dreamgirls *for one dollar.*

In my life I've made many choices and I stand by all of them. As I've said, my Diva friends, life is choices. Choices both big and small all add up to something.

One of those choices I'd made—a big one—wouldn't arrive until many years later. Despite the monetary gain from thousands of productions and a big-budget movie, I chose *not* to go back and seek financial gain for my participation in the creation of *Dreamgirls.*

I have a great deal of respect for the choice to seek

compensation by many of the original contributors to *A Chorus Line*. I admire their strength in seeking what they felt they were owed, and I understand them more than they could possibly know, but at some point I decided, for better or worse, that choice *was not for me*.

But in case you are wondering, let me set the record straight from my point of view. What it comes down to is this: *Deena Jones, the character I created in* Dreamgirls, *is very much a part of me. She comes from me. She would not exist as she is without my input.*

Dreamgirls is a musical that we—meaning the actors as much as the writers and director—created. And by *created*, I mean we often brought the seed of an idea to life.

Dreamgirls began with no script. At the start, there were just the cast in a room with Tom Eyen and sometimes Henry Krieger. They would give us options for songs and scenes within their concept. We took those ideas and spent hours doing improvisations that were recorded and formed into rough scripted material and music. We would build from those rough scenes and work them into the magic they became. This ongoing, constantly evolving process of ensemble creation was not unlike that in the creation of *A Chorus Line*.

These characters emerged from the actors, so we knew better than anyone else what these characters would and would not do. If I felt that Deena was doing something within the script that *my* Deena would not do, I let that be known. Since this was a workshop, my thoughts were often taken seriously, and the material would once again be adjusted and rewritten. This would happen again and again, until we had something that resembled the *Dreamgirls* of today.

A great portion of Deena's character and dialogue—as well as the choices she makes and actions she takes throughout the script—are mine. They were birthed from my own experiences as a young black woman wanting nothing more than to share her talent in a big way. Like Deena, I would have struggles. And like Deena, I would survive and thrive through it all.

Of course, at the time I didn't know the "survive and thrive" part of my life was to be so intensely tested in the following months. *Dreamgirls*—both the creation and the run of the show itself—would test me in ways I could never have imagined.

Years later, watching lines I'd written come out of the mouth of Beyoncé on the big screen, well, that was a moment I found both strange and surreal.

No matter what, one thing will never change. I will forever be grateful for what *Dreamgirls* taught me, and the impact that musical had on the world and me. Being part of creating that show—the *Dreamgirls* universe—is something I hold dear. *Dreamgirls* at some point went from belonging to any of us and became something that belonged to—and often inspires—the world.

"We're your Dreamgirls . . . boys, we'll make you happy."

For me, money won't change anything. I just know this: I wouldn't trade that experience—both the ecstasy and the disappointments, the best and the worst moments of my life—for *anything.*

One last thing. All these years, one thought has always been with me. One day I will share my *Dreamgirls* experiences with the world in hopes that they will offer insight and inspiration to those who read them and continue to dream . . . BIG.

And no amount of money in the world is more important than that.

And this is one of the reasons I wrote this book.

The first thing Michael Bennett did was to search for a talent to fill the shoes of Nell Carter. Effie "Melody" White would not be an easy character to cast. Tom Eyen—always on the lookout for his Effie—went to see the musical *Your Arms Too Short to Box with God*. Jamie Patterson was in the *Dreamgirls* workshop and knew the lead in the other musical. He became instrumental in the discovery of Jennifer and bringing her to Tom's attention.

Jennifer Holliday was a huge talent from a small town in Texas, and our experiences mirrored each other's in many ways. Just as in my *Reggae* experience, she'd been cast in her first Broadway show the same day she auditioned. That had been two years earlier, and now she was twenty-one. In so many ways, we were alike. We were both talented, young black girls with intense drive, probably both thrilled and a little scared at the sudden turn our lives had taken.

Unfortunately, we wouldn't have the opportunity to be friends until decades later. During the evolution and first run of *Dreamgirls,* and for years after, we'd be thought of as rivals. People would hear our names and think the word *catfight*.

There is some truth to every rumor. But sometimes the real truth lies much deeper. Yes, Jennifer and I were rivals, but that choice was made *for* us. We were never allowed to be friends. From moment one, Michael Bennett pitted us against each other. That second workshop would give us a name for the show and the gift of Jennifer Holliday to play Effie, but she left the project after some disapproval of her character and the material. She simply wanted more, and it just wasn't there yet. The workshop was still young. Michael Bennett himself was pretty uncomfortable with the material at this time as it was developing under the direction of Tom Eyen. In those early days, the cast seemed to appear and disappear through a revolving door.

The boisterous Jenifer Lewis joined us for a few weeks when the script was in transition. When she didn't work out, one of the stars of *Hair* was brought in and left just as quickly.

At that point in the show's development, Effie was a home nurse after she left the Dreams. Her character took care of an old Jewish lady played by Estelle Getty, who would go on to play Sophia on *Golden Girls*. S. Epatha Merkerson, later of *Law & Order,* joined us as Jimmy's wife.

Despite the chaos of a rotating cast, I was always around. I was there from the beginning.

The workshops continued. By the fourth workshop, Michael Bennett had taken over as director of the show and promptly changed the name from *Big Dreams* to *Dreamgirls*. In the fourth workshop we sat around a table deconstructing and reconstructing the story. We were moved from a fifties-era show to a sixties-era show. Michael Bennett wooed Jennifer Holliday back to the table.

The rest is, as they say, theater history . . . or the beginning of theater history, at least.

* * *

I had a long, emotionally turbulent relationship with the infamous Michael Bennett. Michael was a creative genius, and a gift to the world of musical theater. He was a legend, and his vision will live on as each new generation discovers his masterful work.

That said, he wasn't the easiest man in the world to deal with. And I'm putting that mildly.

But the truth, my soon-to-be-full-fledged divas, is this: *in your lifetime, you'll dance with many different kinds of people. And I guarantee some of them will step on your toes.*

How will you deal with these people? Well, this took years for me to learn, and I'm still learning. But without a doubt, working with Michael Bennett was a crash course.

9

A Diva Deals with
Difficult People

One of the main characters in *A Chorus Line* is Zach, the director character who is running an audition where he must pare down seventeen hopefuls to eight cast members. In doing so, he often berates and manipulates the actors, pushing them as far as he possibly can. He wants to see how well they handle stress. He is a perfectionist who thrives by pressuring others to perform to his idea of artistic perfection. He is capable of tenderness, but those moments are rare. This character is flawed, tough, and absolutely brilliant.

Just as the auditioning actors in *A Chorus Line* were based on real interviews, the director character came from real life as well, being based on Michael Bennett himself. So that notoriously tough director who storms down the aisle in the first act and opens the show shouting, "Step, kick, kick, leap, kick, touch . . . Again! Step, kick, kick, leap, kick, touch . . . Again!" as the actors struggle through the difficult choreography? Well, I knew that man—excuse me, *character*—well.

Michael demanded a great deal of us, our time, our talent, and our complete attention to the details of his new masterpiece. I had learned from my first movie, and the great Poitier, to give the director my complete attention. But it seemed to me that Michael thrived in an atmosphere of self-created tension. Drama and conflict were the order of the day. He did everything he possibly could to put a wedge between Jennifer and me. We were both young, naïve, and very aware that we'd been given the greatest opportunity of our lives, and with Michael Bennett at the helm, we knew *Dreamgirls* had a good chance of becoming a huge hit. Michael could find financial backing and the talent to make the show come alive, and we knew he had the power to fire either of us at the drop of a feather boa. Michael wanted us to dislike each other. He'd show blatant favoritism for me one day, Jennifer the next. He would be hot and cold to us both, often comparing us in front of the cast and even worse, to each other.

One moment I'll never forget that says it all was on *opening night*. Michael Bennett gave the cast gifts. For Jennifer: Tiffany diamond earrings. For me: a silver-plated belt buckle with the *Dreamgirls* logo on it. A nice gift, but certainly not a girl's best friend.

I know this was a small thing, but to this day, the small thing often means a great deal. It hurts me now just as much as it did then.

For years I've tried to understand Michael's motivation in creating an atmosphere of tension between his real-life leading ladies. Since the Deena and Effie characters became rivals— both fighting for the limelight and at one point the same man—perhaps Michael felt this tension would transfer well to the stage.

Or maybe he just liked the drama.

Either way, the atmosphere was thick with uneasiness. Because the show was still evolving, Michael would regularly adjust the script. Sometimes I'd be given the juicier solos, just to have them snatched away and all attention given to Jennifer.

As we grew more connected to the project, and the story began to take its final shape, we *became* these characters. We loved, fought, and hoped for their success, as well as the success of the show itself. Michael could have moments of supportiveness toward us, but just as often we lived in uneasiness and fear. Perhaps this mythical catfight between Jennifer and me—one that we've discussed at length and even found humorous now as adult women—has somehow become prophetic.

A common belief was that the same catfight existed between Jennifer Hudson and Beyoncé as they were making *Dreamgirls* the movie almost thirty years later.

There might have been drama backstage, but what happened onstage was much clearer. We all knew the show was something special. You could feel that magic in the air. But the real question that haunted us was, would this show ever have an audience? We still didn't have full financial backing.

Michael Bennett took to the street to find someone who believed in Project 9 enough to fund the production. He partnered with David Geffen, a shrewd, handsome young man with the most beautiful piercing blue eyes. David Geffen signed up to be one of the producers and brought in another big name, Quincy Jones.

At that time, no one was bigger than Quincy. He was the man behind Michael Jackson. Quincy Jones could snap his fingers and we'd have a real, bona fide Broadway show on our hands.

Michael told us Q—that's what he called him—was coming to see a complete run-through of the first act. We were so excited. This was a black man with power. Any issues Jennifer and I were having, we put them aside. Quincy arrived and we waited giddily in the rooms of 890 Broadway with our fingers crossed. "This is it," I whispered to sweet Loretta Devine.

"Ralph, I have a good feeling," she whispered back. We both grinned at each other. I said a silent prayer, and I'm sure she did too.

Quincy was a tallish, good-looking man. He sat in the back of the room with Michael and David looking at the show as it played out on the huge Mylar screens before us. It was going so well. Everybody was on point. And then we went right into the scene with Jennifer's gut-wrenching rendition of "And I Am Telling You." We had rehearsed and rehearsed for this moment, all for Mr. Jones's visit.

I remember thinking how great we all were doing, and how amazed Mr. Jones must be with what we'd created. *This is the beginning of everything,* I thought to myself.

Then it happened. As soon as we reached the point where Effie sings, "Cause baby, baby, you're driving me wild!" and the chorus chimed in with "Showbiz, just showbiz" . . . well, Quincy Jones stood up. Just like that, he stood up and *walked right out of our rehearsal.* Not a word of warning, not a word of anything, not even a thank-you and good-bye. Quincy had exited the building. All I remember is my shock as I saw the back of that expensive suit disappear out the door. David Geffen followed right behind.

I turned to Loretta and Jennifer. "But we were good!" I said. They were just as confused as I was.

"He didn't get it," Michael Bennett told me later. *He didn't get it?!*

"But we're going to be big!" I said, almost crying. Michael just shook his head at me. Once again, I was that little girl Nell Carter had seen. The girl who knew nothing about the real world.

It's just showbiz, I guess.

I'd see Mr. Jones again. Years later I was asked to sing as part of a Peggy Lee tribute at the Hollywood Bowl. My song was "Big Spender," and I sang my heart out in my own particular style to the crowd of thousands underneath those stars. After the show, Quincy came up to me and said, "You really let it all out tonight. You're very talented."

I don't think he had any idea of that moment we'd shared long ago or that we'd ever met before. When he'd first seen me in the *Dreamgirls* workshop, I'd been nothing more than a young, eager woman desperate to impress him. I am sure he'd encountered so many others like me.

"Thank you," I said. And I meant it. We all make mistakes.

We didn't let Quincy stop us. We kept right at it. We knew that Project 9—or *Dreamgirls*—was extraordinary. It had to happen; we figured someone would eventually see the magic and want to help us.

Then we got the news that Michael had secured the funding. Our little underdog show about a trio of young black women with big dreams who go from being nobodies to having everything, losing some of the important things on the way to fame . . . well, it was headed for the Great White—or maybe Great Black, in this case—Way.

My life would never again be the same.

10

A Diva Has Good Days . . .
and Bad Ones

*L*ooking back, starring in *Dreamgirls* on Broadway gave me some of the best times in my life. It also gave me some of the most horrific.

No one is born a Diva, my friends. A real Diva becomes DIVA through experience. A real Diva—that *divinely inspired, vivaciously alive* woman whose roots come from the Latin word for *goddess*—is not born a Diva. She is born with the potential for Divahood, and getting there isn't always easy. Real Divas—like everybody else—have their highs and lows. Real Divas make mistakes, but real Divas—*the kind we are, my friends*—can stumble gracefully on the road of life.

I was barely in my twenties and I was starring on Broadway. In the next few years, I'd have moments of triumph unlike any I could have imagined. I'd have those stumbles too.

Some of those stumbling moments would turn into outright trips ending in a fall. The best Diva training of all was learning to get up, dust myself off, and just keep moving forward on the road of life.

* * *

When Broadway history is being made, you can feel it, read the *New York Times* on December 21, 1981.

My life changed overnight.

We were a smash success. It was the most exciting time I can remember. In some ways, the experience is a blur of images and emotions. There we were on that grand stage of the Imperial Theatre. The audiences were right there with us. They rose to their feet night after night. They showered us with the kind of applause that lets you know that you are loved, really truly loved.

This revolutionary musical starring black women was a hit the likes of which Broadway hadn't seen in years. We went from praying for backers and believers to sold-out houses with a year of advance ticket sales. Our pictures were splashed on magazine covers and newsstands across New York, London, and even Tokyo. There were television appearances and rave reviews.

Our show had touched people with freshness and original-ity. *Dreamgirls* spoke to anyone who ever had a dream. Anyone who ever had big hopes and even bigger obstacles. This was a show about making your way and succeeding, even if the world told you it was impossible.

That was a message that seemed to reach people. Fans ranged from children seeing their first musical to young women finding their own dreams to gay men who secretly wanted to be a member of the Dreams. The stay-at-home mati-nee mom to the A-list movie star . . . everybody found some-thing to love in *Dreamgirls*.

Dreamgirls had exploded. We were the toast of the town,

the belles of the ball on Broadway. We had our celebrity fans, such as Michael Jackson, who came to see the show again and again. Luther Vandross was in that audience more times than I even remember. He went from being a fan to a friend. And he remained a great friend until the time of his passing.

I would be in the show for a little over a year, but I would have a lifetime of experiences. This would be one of the most magical, confusing times of my life.

This was the beginning of a crazy time in New York. This was the height of the Studio 54 days, and I was invited everywhere. Lavish engagements and gorgeous dinner affairs took place after the show. I was welcomed with open arms by people—sometimes white people—who would never have given a black woman the time of day before they saw *Dreamgirls*.

Legendary parties were held at Michael Bennett's Central Park South apartment. Everyone wanted to be there—celebrities, politicians, famous actors, and musicians. You felt lucky to get an invitation. However Michael was feeling about me at the time, I was often invited. *Dreamgirls* was his prize show after all, and he called me "one of *my* stars." If anything, he liked to show off his "stars" as a physical manifestation of his success.

I will never forget those parties. You never knew what to expect. Would it be a straight crowd or a gay crowd? Businessmen and their mistresses? Hollywood A-listers? Rich men with their beautiful young trophy boys? Cougars and their hot young bucks?

The whole experience was overwhelming and eye-opening.

And then there was the sudden reality of a world I'd never really seen before. There was sex and drugs. The two can be a dangerous mixture. Add a little alcohol for an extra kick on the elevator ride down.

In my wildest imagination I could never have pictured the amount of cocaine I saw at parties all across Manhattan, all for the taking or sniffing. It would often be elegantly presented, piled high like miniature snow mountains on silver trays. Beautiful people would cut it with the precision of artists and arrange lines so fast their hands were a blur.

Drugs were never my thing. I could still hear Nell Carter saying, "Stay away from the hard stuff." If I was ever tempted, and it was easy to be tempted, I just remembered Nell's face. I just remembered how crack cocaine literally took the beauty and life away from one of my childhood friends. I remembered how unattractive drunk and high girls looked. I remembered what my mother had told me for years: *Don't leave your drink anywhere . . . ever! If you smoke, you'll ruin your voice and smell bad, and never, ever put anything up your nose.* I'm not sure how I stayed so strong with all those people pushing drugs on me, but somehow I did. And this crowd—full of people who influenced audiences for a living—well, they could be *persistent.* But I kept thinking, *I got a show to do tomorrow.*

Being strong in the face of this kind of temptation would be hard, but it would only be the first of many tests.

I understand those young Hollywood stars and the temptations they face because I faced them all. I was young, after all, and suddenly thrust into the limelight.

Lord knows I made some stupid choices. And—not surprisingly—some of those stupid choices involved men.

I had plenty of admirers. All sorts of men came out of the woodwork to date a real live Dreamgirl. Some pursued me intensely, but I was picky. Not to mention that I hardly had time to sleep with eight grueling shows a week. So dating and parties were not my first priority.

Of course, that didn't stop me, and I'm just as susceptible to a handsome face as any woman in her early twenties. God knows I had my pick. Starring in a hit Broadway show meant I was never at a lack for suitors and admirers. But were they interested in me—Sheryl Lee Ralph—or the sexy siren Deena Jones? *That* was the question. Yes, a great deal of myself was in the character of Deena. As her popularity soared through the course of the musical, my own journey in real life was mirroring her experiences. But Deena and I were very different as well. She had decades of experience to live and learn from in every two-and-a-half-hour show . . . when I stepped out that stage door every night, I was still in my early twenties and in some ways more innocent than my years.

Of course, I didn't say no to *every* stage-door Johnny. I dated quite a few handsome men. There was the famous musician who'd get recognized wherever we went, but he was kind of kinky and I just couldn't keep up with all that. The television actor who was almost too attractive for his own good, sometimes getting distracted by his *own* reflection in shop windows when we walked down the street. I had to laugh at it 'cause it was fun and funny, though I never took any of those guys too seriously.

And I'm glad I didn't because these were the eighties, when playing musical beds was as accepted as playing Monopoly. But all that would suddenly change when sex became synonymous with death. The AIDS epidemic hit Broadway with a thud we still feel to this day. In a short time, everything would change forever.

Looking back now, I'm glad I took my time, because sleeping—or hooking up, for my younger Divas—with someone too quickly is the fastest way to mess up what could be a meaningful relationship. A Diva knows her worth . . . *and she's worth waiting for.* If the person really matters to you, take your time and give it time.

On some level I knew that even then, but as the old saying goes, when love is the last thing you are looking for, it might just tap you on the shoulder and say, "Here I am, honey."

Then I met someone. An advertising executive. He saw me perform, he sent me flowers and a gift. I said yes to a date with a man more than twenty-five years my senior.

Now here's the thing about dating pretty young things, especially those in the public eye . . . they don't always know who they are *themselves* yet. They can be surrounded by publicists and agents, fans and yes-men, an entourage of people who make a living off their success. Many of them start in showbiz early and never have the opportunity to live regular young lives before they become a "name" or the next hot thing. That combination of success, insecurity, and a staff telling you that you are the greatest thing since sliced bread? That can be a recipe for disaster. We have seen it happen over and over with the same results.

And here is this sophisticated older man, courting me. And the first thing that struck me is that he *knew* himself.

He knew who he was as a man. He was successful, and he'd worked hard for his success. He'd seen the world and had real-life experiences my young mind couldn't begin to fathom. He'd traveled. He wasn't a boy. And, yes, he was handsome, and not in the "pretty" way I was used to with the man-boys I'd been seeing. This man entered a room and *owned* it. He was dashing and well-spoken. We could have an actual conversation, and he was interested in my views on the world and had things he could teach me.

Oh, yeah, and the part I haven't mentioned was that he treated me like an *absolute princess*. In his eyes, I was a treasure. I should be handled carefully, adored and fully appreciated at every moment even if I was only ten years older than his daughter.

As should you, my Diva friends. If you work hard on yourself to achieve a Diva-worthy level of confidence and stature, well, you'll know you're *worth* that adoration and pick people who are suitably appreciative of you. They'll know *they are blessed to be with you* and so will *you*. You should be loved.

This man had money—*real* money—and he wasn't afraid to spoil me. These were the kind of dates you only read about in romance novels. A limo waiting for me after a show to whisk me off to a private table in the most luxurious, exclusive restaurants in the city. The kind with a six-month waiting list to get in. Sudden surprise trips on my rare days off, to a private island where his chef would cook us delicious meals and we'd walk on our own beach at sunset. You can't make this stuff up.

I was completely, utterly taken with the whole experience. I thought I was head-over-Manolo-Blahniks in love. Of course, my brain might have been a little clouded.

That was the beginning of a truly important Diva lesson: *a Diva deserves to feel good in all aspects of life, from the bedroom to the boardroom and every place in between.* And a real man—one worthy of a Diva—is not afraid to make sure she feels real good.

So maybe it was infatuation, but I truly believed I'd found my prince charming. We saw each other for quite a while, and everyone could see me changing. Even onstage, I'd feel this man's presence and channeled all that emotion into Deena. When Deena sang her love, well, that was Sheryl Lee Ralph singing her own.

I was so happy. Still, I was relatively inexperienced in the reality of relationships. While my college friends had been looking to get married, I'd been looking toward my career and getting my stardom on. While other actors in LA had been living the swinging eighties lifestyle, I'd *still* been looking toward my career. And now I was in my early twenties, and this was my first serious love affair. Needless to say, I didn't yet know how to read all the signals.

When I got too close, he'd back away. The scenario repeated itself. We'd get closer, and then he'd stop returning my calls.

But I was seeing the world through a filter of young love, and I'd keep calling. You've been there. *Admit it.* I continued to let him make plans—and cancel them on me. It was the classic bad-boyfriend scenario, and I'd have to break that cycle. It took my truly valuing myself to know when to walk away. Now that sounds good, but the truth is, in the end, he actually pushed me away from him.

He knew I was the marrying kind, and at this point I fully owned that I *lived* to be a mother one day. That was not at all what he wanted. He had his children and was set in not wanting any more, and he had taken steps to make sure that it did not happen. A family—and an adoring younger girlfriend—was not in the cards. During another fantasy date he set the scene for the breakup. *You deserve to have the joy of motherhood and you won't get that with me.*

He was right. Still, I was willing to give up that dream to be with him.

"So this is where it ends," he said, dropping the keys to our beautiful suite in my hands. And with those keys, I felt my heart drop too. "Enjoy the weekend. The room is paid for." To this day the rest of what he said to me is a blur.

I was devastated and depressed. I had just been dumped. Even though he dumped me in the lap of luxury, it didn't hurt any less. Painful experiences that will mold you into a stronger woman. Of course, when you're eating a pint or two of Häagen-Dazs with tears rolling down your face, it feels as if the world is coming to an end. But it *won't,* my Diva friends. I *promise.* When I look at the two beautiful children I have today, I thank God that he dumped me.

Cry it out! Vent, pray, wish! Then get out of bed and start all over again. Put on a pretty dress, a fresh coat of mascara, and go out and face the world!

Something even better is right around the corner. Do not dwell on it . . . too long. Let it be lipstick and lashes under the bridge, my Diva.

I always dated for love, not money or material goods. I have seen all those women who dated men thinking they were going to get something. Some became the baby mama thinking it would make him stay. All that just wasn't my style. Some actresses date to further their careers. That might open the door, but you better have the guts and talent to stay in the room. Not to mention, you have to be careful. The industry is not always pretty, and there's always the risk you'll end up folded in a suitcase and out with the trash.

For better or worse—better, I truly believe—I was looking for my love story. Unfortunately, sometimes the love story doesn't end the way it does in the fairy tales, and you're left without the glass slipper, crying yourself to sleep, wondering why you keep falling for the prince's bad-seed brother with commitment issues.

But in the end, you learn. I wouldn't fully understand the signs—or see that I'd been picking the wrong men—until years later. But I would eventually realize, and that would make all the difference. I'd be able to discern charm without the intelligence even if he was fine, gifts given to get something without the appreciation of the real me, guys who could talk a good game but would duck and run at crunch time. Now I know those are signs that a guy is *just wrong*.

I look at my husband now and see a man with genuine

kindness, a big heart, and a love for me that is true and comes from an appreciation for who I am at my core. I look at him and know he'll take me for better or worse and love me through the good and the bad. I look at that man and see a great politician who lives to make the world a better place, and a man who knows I am an important part of his well-being, happiness, and success. A man who truly appreciates me for all that I am—the lovely and the complicated—and wouldn't have me any other way. I look at that man and know I am loved and I *deserve* it.

That, my Divas, is what makes all the difference.

11

Divas Have Growing Pains Too

As I look back, my days in *Dreamgirls* were some of the greatest and most challenging of my life. For the good times, I am eternally grateful. Having the opportunity to reach audiences every night—to see their faces light up with joy as they watched us, to move them to tears, to touch them and lift them and give them hope—was a *gift*. Being part of such an iconic show was a blessing.

Dreamgirls was revolutionary. Finally there was a stage full of beautifully black women. They weren't stereotypes or background characters, they were the show itself. To be a part of something so ahead of its time—and something that would open the door to young black actresses everywhere—is something I'm proud to have been a part of.

But part of opening doors that have never been opened . . . well, it isn't always pretty on the other side.

Those early *Dreamgirls* days would offer a lifetime of lessons, and some of those lessons would be painful. More wake-up calls would occur in that short span than most women have in their entire twenties.

I'd always been overly trusting of people. I'd been raised with a community who looked out for me and believed in heartfelt kindness. Even through difficult experiences in Hollywood I'd kept faith that people were genuinely good at heart. They struggled as we all do, but if they said they wanted the best for you, well, they *meant* it.

That, my Diva friends, is an unfortunate lesson because it isn't always true. You have to *find* the good people, the ones who really want the best for you, and hold them close. And getting fooled, well, that is part of learning how to find them.

Dreamgirls taught me some early lessons about sisterhood. And they weren't always easy to learn.

My mother taught me the importance of sisterhood. I'm a proud member of Delta Sigma Theta. Watching my sorority sisters go out into the world and triumph is extremely satisfying. Their successes are mine. There is power in belonging to a community of women whose work and beliefs you respect. Having women with whom to speak your mind is vital to staying emotionally sane, and any Diva knows, *if Mama don't feel good, nobody feels good*.

Backstabbing, demeaning, trying to undermine the success of your sisters, well, it seems plain crazy to me. That is why I celebrate all women who celebrate sisterhood. No matter what colors they wear. Crimson and cream, pink and green, blue and white, blue and gold, and any combination thereof. I celebrate *sisterhood*.

Black women have always had to work harder than anyone else. We left the African continent under pain and duress and were put to backbreaking work throughout the American continent. This is what we did, do, and are . . . *working* women.

We did our share—more than our share—and then kept going because we didn't have a choice. When our great-great-grandmothers were out there working in those fields—and they happened to be pregnant—well, they didn't have a choice. They couldn't take time off to recharge. There was no maternity leave. They dropped those babies in the hot sun, wrapped them up, strapped them to their backs, and resumed work. They didn't have time for petty worries or nasty behavior, they had better things to do. Such as *survive*.

Those are the women we come from. This is our legacy and I'd been taught not to forget that. You shouldn't forget it either. Someone picked cotton for my dream to come true. And here I was on a grander stage—*literally*—than I could ever have imagined. There were so few roles for black women out there, and I'd landed one of the best. And not every woman in the entertainment industry was thrilled for me about it.

But I truly believe that when women work together and support each other, there is a lot of power in that. And that kind of power can change the world for the better.

The discomfort that lingered between Jennifer and me would not have existed without Michael Bennett's favoritism and controlling antics. But another woman out there had become my adversary, despite that we had never really met and I'd admired her for as long as I could remember.

Word got back to me—and the rest of the cast—that Miss Diana Ross was not happy with us. She was angry at what she believed was my portrayal of her. She wasn't afraid to tell everyone she met—including the major publications—that she felt our show was a blatant rip-off of her own rise to stardom.

Dreamgirls was *her story,* she said. And she said it very publicly.

No matter how many times I said that I was not playing Diana Ross, the urban legend grew. I'd always worshipped Miss Ross, but I knew that our story was completely original. Project 9 was based on the pure creativity of actors around a table in those early workshops. The cast's experiences—our own highs and lows—were the emotional center of the script. Not to mention, there was the perfect plot for every great musical or movie—boy meets girl, boy loses girl, and boy gets her back again. A journey that speaks to us all.

As for the rise to stardom being Diana's story? Well, of course she could relate to it. It was the story of so many young, gifted black girls with big talent and even bigger dreams. It was the story that created Motown and the Sound of Philadelphia. Yes, the Supremes were in there, but so were the Shirelles and the Three Degrees and many, many other black, gifted female singers who fought to get the recognition they deserved. This story was our legacy as black performers, and the legacy of the brave pioneers who brought R&B and soul music to the world.

Mary Wilson of the Supremes understood that and embraced the show as something to be proud of. Though she admitted that some moments felt familiar, she has been very public in her belief that *Dreamgirls* is a work of art, and an excellent one at that. She's still so proud of *Dreamgirls* that she often tells me, "Sheryl Lee Ralph, I'm the original Dreamgirl," with a big smile spread across her face. "No," I'd say. "You're the original *Supreme, I* am the original *Dreamgirl.*" I love Mary, and either way, we are both proud of having been part of something iconic.

As the story goes, after Mary Wilson published her highly successful memoir, *Dreamgirl: My Life as a Supreme,* Diana

Ross was not happy with the attention Mary was getting. The whole thing led to some sort of altercation at the 25th Motown anniversary show. According to Wilson and numerous witnesses of the incident, Ross pushed Wilson while they both stood onstage. I wasn't there, so I don't know. But I do know that women have extraordinary power when they've got each other's back, and even more when they choose to knife each other in the back. Being upset because another woman has success says more *about you* than anything else. You might have heard someone utter the phrase "Ummmph, she thinks she's all that!" Well, what that person is really saying is "I am *not* all that!"

Of course I couldn't put that into perspective at that time. All I knew was that one of my icons—Diana Ross—really, really disliked me. It was painful. *Stop,* I wanted to tell her. *In the name of love!*

It's important to remember that a Diva doesn't enter a room saying, "Look at me! Look at me!" A real Diva knows that she is someone *to be looked at.* Either way, *everyone* turned to look at Miss Ross.

I'd heard all the things she'd said about me and the show. I knew how she felt. But I'd adored and admired her since I was a little girl. I had even snuck into her dressing room like little Eve Harrington one summer at the Westbury Music Fair. Not to mention, my father always said I should only *believe half of what you see and none of what you hear.* Sometimes gossip and hearsay is *just that.*

So when she entered the Russian Tea Room when I was there having lunch . . . I was thrilled. Besides, just seeing that gorgeous woman with that huge halo of hair within a few feet of me . . . I think my brain momentarily stopped working. All I could think was *That's Diana Ross! That's really her!*

I stood up and walked right over to her. "Miss Ross!" I said. She stopped and turned around dramatically with that gleaming smile of hers. There she was, the great Miss Diana Ross, for whom I'd stayed up late to watch on the *Ed Sullivan Show,* right there in front of *me.* And she was *stunning.* She seemed to glow.

I had to speak to her. "I'm Sheryl Lee—"

"Ralph," she cut me off instantly. The smile disappeared from her face. It just seemed to *melt clear away.* The whole room went quiet, just like in the movies, or at least it seemed that way.

"*I. Know. Who. You. Are,*" she hissed, glaring at me. "You're from *that show.*" The way she said *that show* was as if she'd just tasted something so horrible that she had to spit it out. Then she gave me a look that put a chill on all the vodka in the Russian Tea Room that afternoon.

With that, she turned on her heels, flipped her huge mane of hair, and walked away from me. *Dreamgirls* would open my eyes to the real world, and sometimes you had to look at it through tears.

I'd see Diana again. I ran into her in Jamaica where she was performing at Air Jamaica's Jazz & Blues Festival. She was with three of her beautiful children. Her youngest son is not only talented but seems to have the heart of an angel. He made sure his mom and I talked. He didn't like this old rivalry, and he went out of his way to make us reintroduce ourselves and chat. After a few seconds of awkwardness, Diana and I found something we both cared about deeply to discuss: our children.

During that conversation, we went from being notorious rivals to something far more important than any show or song.

We were simply two *mothers*. We had a pleasant chat about what really matters and how our children are the loves of our lives. We talked about our pride in nurturing our young to be strong, loving, good adult men and women.

I can give Diana Ross a compliment, and it is the highest compliment I could ever give anyone: she has raised some wonderful children, and that is not easy.

I don't remember the details of petty backstage *Dreamgirls* fights. But what I do remember—and what will forever be ingrained in my consciousness—are the moments that really mattered.

I'd been so excited to get the call that I'd been nominated for the prestigious Antoinette Perry Award (aka the Tony). I immediately called my parents. My mind went into overdrive wondering what I'd wear to the luncheon and whom I'd take as my date.

And this is the power of sisterhood: the moment I found out that we'd all been nominated except for Loretta Devine, a woman with her own brand of divine magic.

Instantly, I went from cloud nine to heartbroken. I wanted to take this walk with her. We'd been on this journey together since the beginning, and my exhilaration was suddenly cut with a sharp sadness. Michael Bennett was so distressed that he threw his own awards party, and that was a wonderful occasion. Being able to celebrate that all that hard work had led to success—and doing so with all the *Dreamgirls* sisters—was the true award.

* * *

Do I remember the specifics of the childish arguments between Jennifer Holliday and me? No, because they were *childish*. We weren't really that far out of girlhood ourselves. But what still makes me glow with pride and will be with me forever? Sitting next to her at the LA premiere of the latest reincarnation of *Dreamgirls* to hit the road. The lights went down in the theater, the show began, and Jennifer took my hand. She whispered, her soft voice full of sincerity, "Sheryl, if we only knew then what we know now."

Yes, and I am telling you, *if only*.

Those are the moments that matter, the ones of friendship and love and bonds that can never be severed. Those are the ones I keep close.

As I said, Divas don't hang on to anger. Let it go and be lipstick and eyelashes under the bridge.

Fame can be a double-edged sword. While our growing success made Diana Ross angry, it seemed to make Michael Bennett uneasy. The more popular we got, the more neurotic he became. Unfortunately, I'd never get the same closure with him that I did with Diana Ross when I saw her in Jamaica.

The more packed houses and rave reviews, the more manipulative Michael turned with the cast. Even moments such as the one with Diana—the devastation of having her speak out against us—was *publicity*. And *publicity* brought in audiences. And the more audiences and acclaim and the higher the box office sales, the more insecure and unstable Michael became. He seemed to unravel, and few would speak out against the genius behind our hit show, especially since he signed, directly or indirectly, most of the paychecks.

Michael continued to turn the actresses against each other and regularly criticize our performances. No matter how popular we got, Michael had a way of making me feel—with one throwaway comment or perfectly timed sneer—that I wasn't good enough. Never mind that we were singing and sweating to packed houses every night, he still took some sort of twisted pleasure in hurting us. For some reason, I was his favorite target. Maybe because—strong-willed as I am—I'd often stand up for myself. I refused to cower under that man's dictatorship. That made him even more furious with me at times.

And it would only get worse.

12

Divahood Ain't Always Easy

*M*ichael Bennett had extraordinary vision. He was progressive and gifted. But here is the unfortunate truth: being a deeply talented artist with the world at your feet does not erase your inner turmoil. A deeply talented artist is also capable of being a deeply flawed human being.

Some believe great art comes from great pain. A traumatic childhood—or the feeling of being an outsider—can be channeled into emotionally powerful works of art. I agree, but only to an extent. Yes, many great artists have felt like outsiders. I was an outsider, and, yes, those feelings have made my work richer. But using that anger as an excuse to treat others badly? Using your own pain like a weapon? Spending your life hurting those around you because you've been hurt yourself?

I believe that is a *choice. And that choice is a bad one.*

What did my grandmother say? Misery loves company. And that is why miserable people spend a lot of time trying to get you to join them in their misery. Grandmother was right then, and it is still true today.

Eventually, the exhilaration of being in a big Broadway show settled a bit. We worked so hard that we were often exhausted. Live theater is one of the most fulfilling and difficult career moves an actor can make, especially when the show is a hit. Night after night of dancing and singing our hearts out was strenuous work. Then you go home, catch a few hours of rest, and get up to do it again the next day.

One of the lowest moments—and a moment that is as clear to me as the day it happened—was when Michael's father came to see the show. Michael's father was an old-school Italian man like those you see in the movies—well dressed, full of swag and machismo. Maybe the visit brought out the machismo in Michael himself. More likely, it brought his deep-seated insecurity to the surface.

Michael was notorious for embracing both his male and female sides. He wanted his father to be proud, and a *gay* son wasn't something his father would easily have embraced. A lot has changed in terms of gay rights since then. Not as much or as quickly as it should have, but at least there is a more wide-spread understanding of homosexuality. But this was the eighties, and few men were out to their family, let alone the world. Some of them were ashamed to tell their friends and family who they were born to be, and that is a terrible thing.

Maybe that's why Michael had married Donna McKechnie, who'd starred as Cassie in *A Chorus Line*. Either she didn't know or thought she could change him, but word on the Broadway circuit was that he'd made her life a living hell before finally leaving her, just as the director left Cassie in *A Chorus Line*.

There's a famous saying about life imitating art, and for Michael Bennett, the two were forever linked. As for life being a stage? Well, he could be incredibly dramatic for sure, and he never lacked a stage on which to perform.

The day his father was coming, we had a lengthy rehearsal. Michael wanted to please his parents, and especially his father, more than anything else. He was frantically reworking the second act, even though we'd been on Broadway for over a year. But that was him, notorious for working the hell out of you and the show.

I was exhausted, annoyed, and sick of being yelled at by this man whose show I'd helped make a success. We ran through the routine again and again, and nothing was good enough. Just as the infamous director character bellows directions at Cassie in the famous *A Chorus Line* sequence—"Don't pop the hip, Cassie! Again! Again!"—Michael was like a rabid dog working himself into a frenzy.

I had a huge boa for the number, and a few times it grazed the ground. "Don't let that boa touch the ground," Michael told me. Who knew that a feather boa would be the thing to finally break that camel's back and push him over the edge?

We did it again and again. And then it happened.

The boa touched the floor.

Michael ran down the aisle in a rage. In a flurry of movement, he stopped the orchestra, jumped on the stage, and walked right over to me. He was right there, all in my face.

"I told you not to let the boa touch the floor!" he screeched.

Then he *hit* me. Smacked me stinging hard across my right arm. I can still feel it to this day.

I will never forget the shock. And humiliation. In all my years as an actress—and all my dealings with difficult people—nothing has ever come close to this.

My own father never hit me. It was beyond my comprehension. For a moment, I was speechless. Everyone was watching. *How dare you hit me,* I thought. Then I took that boa off my shoulder and dropped it right on the floor in front of him.

In complete shock, I walked off the stage. Somehow I found my way to the dressing room. Somehow I changed my clothes and walked out onto Eighth Avenue and Forty-Fifth Street. I picked up a pay phone and dialed Actors' Equity.

My voice sounded as if it belonged to someone else—some lost, scared little girl. "This is Sheryl Lee Ralph. And Michael Bennett just hit me."

After a short pause, the man on the other end of the line simply sighed, then said, "What do you want? A vacation? Two weeks' paid leave? Take one. Stay out as long as you want. As long as you need. Don't worry, he'll pay you." There was another sigh. "Look. Don't feel too bad. You're not the first."

I'm not sure how, but I made it back to my apartment—where no one could see me—before I actually cried.

I have never looked at a feather boa the same way since.

Equity has much stronger rules for the protection of its actors today than in the eighties. This wouldn't have happened today. Michael Bennett would have been brought before the disciplinary committee long before my boa incident. But at the time, I was told to ignore it and pretend it hadn't happened. *Let him calm down and go on with the show.* That was just what I did.

But that incident stayed with me and would be one of many catalysts leading up to a new chapter in my life.

13

A Diva Knows When to Make an Exit

The incident with Michael was awful. But other things—worse than I could imagine—would soon follow. Being hit, as humiliating as it was, would pale in comparison.

During the early part of the *Dreamgirls* run, there were whispers around the Broadway circuit and beyond. A mysterious disease was being discussed in hushed voices. This disease seemed to be specifically striking the gay community. It came on suddenly, and men started dropping dead up and down Broadway.

Gay men were a huge part of the success of *Dreamgirls*. Conceiving the show, writing the show, writing the music for the show, producing the show, designing the wigs, buying tickets in record numbers . . . so many dedicated gay men loved *Dreamgirls*. To this day, gay men will discuss the first time they saw *Dreamgirls* and dissolve into tears and smiles. Gay men always loved their dreams, as in The Dreams. I have a theory about that. I think that inside every gay man—no matter his color—is a black woman trying to get out.

Ultimately, *Dreamgirls* is about the struggle for acceptance. Three women from the wrong side of the tracks; because of their color, no one values their talent. Because of their gender, no one values their talent. They rise above it all and make the whole world love them one song at a time.

Gay men saw hope in that. They were some of our biggest fans and supporters, and, on a personal level, some of my closest friends. Nearing the end of my *Dreamgirls* run, those whispers of an unnamed disease had grown into a deadly silence. Nobody wanted to talk about that "gay" disease.

It happened so quickly. It seemed as if overnight this mysterious disease blew out the flame of life on Broadway like candles on a birthday cake. Funeral after funeral. Memorial after memorial. One right after the other, and there didn't appear to be an end in sight. I got to the point where I felt physically ill as I crossed out another name in my address book.

There was no HIV back then, just AIDS. I remember when it had no name. It was called GRID—gay-related immune-deficiency disease. They called it the gay men's cancer. It was a different time, before so many men and women—black, white, gay, and straight—had come out as having been infected by this disease that did not discriminate, just infected and ultimately killed. No one knew the truth yet . . . the truth was AIDS, and it was horrible.

I stood witness to such an ugly time in America, and it forever changed me. It was a time when good people, kind people,

people of all religions and faiths and beliefs, took comfort in passing judgment and pointing fingers. *Those people. Those gay people got what they deserved. God will take care of them.*

Such an ugly time, when people disowned and abandoned their sick and dying children, dumping them on church steps like bags of used clothing for a rummage sale. Families ignoring their own flesh and blood in the time of their greatest need.

My friends were dying one right after the other. Michael Peters, our übertalented choreographer, died. This is the man who helped to create Michael Jackson's signature "Thriller" dance moves, a revolutionary genius that changed the face of dance. And the last time I saw him, there he was hobbling down Seventh Avenue on a cane. Neuropathy had ruined his beautiful feet.

This was long before we had revolutionary treatments for HIV. There was no cocktail, but there was a lot of false information. Some said *you could get it from a sneeze. From a toilet seat. From a kiss.* And once you got it, well, that was it for so many. Some of the men wasted away, some lost their minds to dementia, and some had their bodies morph into some strange shapes with lipodystrophy. But they all had one thing in common: deterioration came fast and furious.

Michael Peters's numb and heavy feet—along with his inability to move without great pain—was a side effect of AIDS. A dancer unable to defy gravity or leap through the air . . . unable to dance! It was the most horrible thing I could imagine, like a singer without his or her voice.

This was after his *Dreamgirls* fame and the iconic moves he'd created with Jackson. Michael Peters was considered one of the most innovative choreographers in America, adored in so many circles.

I hadn't seen him in a long time. That vibrant, energetic, fit man had been transformed into a thin, pale, sickly one. His feet were like lead weights beneath him. I respected Michael Peters enormously—both the man and his talent— but he hadn't always made my life easy. Perhaps his own stress, coupled with the pressure of working for a man as difficult as Michael Bennett, explained why he had often been so unkind to me. But seeing someone in his condition puts things in perspective. I felt my heart drop into my stomach. I forced myself not to burst into tears. I wanted to stay strong, at least for his sake.

He took me completely off guard when he looked me squarely in my eyes. He said softly, "Sheryl Lee, I'm sorry." I knew those words hadn't come easily for him. I appreciated his saying it. But in retrospect, there was something more there. He was sorry how he'd treated me, of course. He was sorry he was dying. But beyond that—and I didn't realize it at the time—he was sorry for *me*.

The truth was obvious. As all my friends had grown sick, I'd grown sick right along with them. Michael saw that—in all the darkness and silence—I was finding my voice. He must have foreseen that I'd use it to speak up for the friends I had lost and would lose in the years to come.

He knew it wouldn't be easy for me.

Michael knew what I didn't know. People would call me crazy and tell me to shut up. Even the sick themselves would tell me it was a waste of my time and not the disease I "a star" should talk about. But Michael knew that wouldn't stop me. He knew exactly how stubborn and driven I could be.

And let me tell you, he was right about it not being easy.

Eventually, Michael Bennett himself would die of AIDS. At that moment—despite the death and fear—we all knew that we had to keep going. We were professionals.

Maybe Michael Bennett already knew this himself, I'm not sure. But his behavior toward his cast continued to worsen.

I look back and can feel sympathy for Michael Bennett. He was so pained within himself. Deep inside, he was that little boy who just wanted his father to be proud of him, the little boy who could never be the version of the "man" his father wanted. Instead of taking comfort in his exceptional gifts—that he was the kind of man to change the world with his artistic vision—he'd kept that hurt little boy inside himself all that time. He wanted to make others feel as bad as he did.

Between the illness that surrounded me and the constant berating from Michael, I felt as if I had no control. What had been one of the highest points in my life had taken a startling turn. *Dreamgirls* had really been a dream come true, and suddenly it began to feel like a nightmare from which I couldn't wake up. Then, one day, something weird happened.

I just stopped eating.

I got to the point where I could go a whole day on some matzo ball soup and a few pieces of fruit. I got smaller and smaller. The transformation happened quickly but I couldn't see it. When I looked in the mirror, I saw a smiling giant. I guess, in my mind, I wanted to disappear. The more Michael treated me unkindly, the less I ate. Now I was the one in control.

But what was I in control of? I was miserable. I had been raised with kindness and was used to nice people. I remember when I was a little girl, my grandmother used to grow flowers. She liked to keep them all the same height. If one flower grew too tall, no matter how pretty it was, it would get cut down to blend evenly with the rest. This new, smaller girl I had become had been cut off. But I wasn't a flower, I was a person.

I had seen that people had the capability for true cruelty, and I'd treat myself like an overgrown flower that didn't match. Off with her head!

During Project 9, I'd felt insanely lucky. Every day I counted my blessings—*here I was, helping to create this innovative show!* Every day I walked into the rehearsal hall, Tom Eyen asked the same question: "How are you?"

I'd smile widely, so happy to be in that room, and say, "Wonderful! I'm wonderful. How are you?"

Sometimes he'd just snicker as if to say, *She's strange but I like her.* He loved that so much he even put it in the show. During the press-conference scene, as Deena ascends to stardom, the paparazzi ask her how she feels with all her success. She responds, "Wonderful, what can I say but wonderful."

That was me. I'd been that girl, but something had changed. That elation had morphed into something far from wondrous.

The woman I'd become felt lost and out of control. Not eating made me feel strangely powerful. I got smaller and smaller. Then one day my costumes weren't fitting. Everyone watched, looking at me as if I were crazy. But I knew I wasn't crazy. *After all,* I thought, *I'm in charge of it.* I must have been so unhappy. At that point I was a size two, which, on my body, made me look pretty skeletal.

Michael Bennett saw my weight changing. He ordered me to eat. He had trays of food sent to the dressing room. The more he told me to eat, the more I wouldn't. Nobody—especially *that man*—was going to tell me what to do.

At that time, there was no common word for what I was doing. Just as AIDS had yet to be properly named, anorexia wasn't part of the public consciousness. But just as with AIDS, that didn't keep it from existing.

I'd always been confident and comfortable in my body. But now I looked in the dressing room mirrors and thought, *Wow, I'm huge.* We were all struggling. A cast becomes a family, and as in any family, dysfunction can grow and fester. As I got smaller, Jennifer seemed to get larger. She'd always struggled with her weight, and she coped with the stress by eating. I coped by not eating, but it was the same thing.

Jennifer probably felt the same way I did. I knew I couldn't fix all the madness, but I could take care of Sheryl Lee. I could control her body and what went in it.

I wasn't a real Diva yet. Obviously, I had years of training in store. But for better or worse, I had one Diva lesson already seared in my brain: *I wouldn't let anyone tell me what to do if I didn't think it was right.*

Only, at that point, I didn't have enough nourishment to think straight, let alone know the difference between wrong and right.

I just kept shrinking.

Of course, the show went on. Playing a lead in a rigorous Broadway musical night after night is hard enough, and doing it without any food in your stomach is almost impossible. Not to mention *foolish*. It takes a toll on your voice when you are so weak. But I wasn't thinking. I was trying to take control. My head was hurting . . . all the time. But I just kept going, and I was there rain or shine. I took my place center stage and stood tall.

Until the day I couldn't stand anymore.

Michael Bennett decided that I was out of the show until further notice. He made arrangements for me to go to a health farm in upstate New York to rest and be fed. I was devastated. I had no say in the matter. There was nothing for me to say.

A car had been arranged and I was to leave at the end of the show that night. The curtain came down and I walked out the stage door.

Then everything went dark.

The next thing I remember is opening my eyes and my mother was stroking my hair. My father was there too. They were holding my hands and doing their best to disguise their horror at my shrunken appearance. "Mommy? Daddy?" I said.

In that moment, something changed. As strong as I'd been—as much as I'd grown up in the past year and found my way in the world—I felt like a little girl. In that moment, I was five years old. I was hurt and I just wanted my mommy. And here she was with my dad too, and I was so, so happy to see them.

"You're going to be fine, Sheryl," she said in that reassuring musical accent. "Everything will be fine now."

"Mommy," I said, tears streaming down my face. After all those months of stress and fear, my mom's face was a beacon of light breaking through the gloom. In her face I saw what I'd somehow forgotten—*I was strong.* I'd been that same girl who—*not so long ago, really*—walked into that Rutgers theater and said, "My name is Sheryl Lee Ralph and I'd like to audition."

That strong, driven, fearless girl was still inside me. I'd just misplaced her for a while. But I'd find her again, and she'd be back to the way she was . . . in fact, she'd be even stronger.

There will be lows, my Diva friends. There always are. *But the test of a true Diva is in how she rises.*

My parents took me to a health clinic to rest, eat, and, most important, find that inner strength I'd lost. Being away that short time gave me perspective. *They* gave me perspective.

All the Tony nominations and starring roles in the world will never replace the love of your family, whether that be the family you are born with or the one you choose or the one you create. Besides nourishment for my body, I needed nourishment for my soul. Being with the people I loved and who loved me—people who would love me had I never gotten a role in my life, had there never been a *Dreamgirls* at all—that was exactly what I needed. I was reminded of *what really mattered*. Or, I guess, *who* would be more accurate.

I went back to the show two weeks later. I wasn't 100 percent physically, but I was a million times stronger emotionally. When you hit a low and find your way back up, sometimes the view looks different.

Maybe it was the energy I was putting out in the world— or maybe word had spread that I'd taken a break from the show—but a few months after I got back there was a call from Hollywood. They were casting a new series called *V,* which has recently been remade for TV. At that time, the show was unique. Not only was it meant to be a hip sci-fi show on network TV, but there were some juicy roles for women. The female sergeant character, tough as nails, could handle two machine guns at the same time. Someone had seen me as Deena and thought I'd be perfect in the part. Go figure!

They didn't outright offer me the part, but Tim Flack, NBC casting director, said I'd have a really good chance if I came to LA and auditioned.

I still wasn't sure. Then something happened that made up my mind. And it happened onstage, of all places.

I forgot my lines.

I went onstage all dolled up with the infamous big feather boa to do "One Night Only." We'd done the show over a thousand times. It wasn't as though the lyrics were that complicated, either. *One night only . . . one night only . . .*

And then I went blank.

For the life of me, I couldn't remember the rest of the song. Backstage, they thought my mike was dead . . . but it wasn't. My *brain* had gone dead. Loretta tried to help me through the song. She tried to cover for me, but the whole experience was a shock.

Maybe the opportunity of an audition in LA had distracted me. It had been more than a year, and maybe it was my mind telling me I'd been doing the show *too long*. Whatever it was, I figured I better listen.

A week later, I knew what I had to do. After the last show of the week, I stood with my lead cast members after the curtain came down. I looked at them. Ben Harney, who played Curtis Taylor Jr. with a mix of love and steely determination. A man of deep kindness who would, not surprisingly, go on to become a man of God. The gifted Cleavant Derricks, who played James "Thunder" Early as no one has since. My talented sisters—Loretta, Jennifer—who had been there at my side every night. Looking at them, and the many others who'd earned a place in my heart, I almost couldn't say what I knew I must.

It hadn't been easy. We'd fought and cried and celebrated and leaned on each other. Most of all, there was *love* there. Just like the song, we *were family*.

But the time had come for me to leave.

I told them it was my last show. I said I was going to Hollywood.

They looked at me as if I were out of my mind. "You're coming back, right?" said Loretta with a devastated expression.

I shook my head.

"She'll be back," I heard a cast member mutter in a not-too-subtle "stage whisper" when I finally got the strength to exit. But I'm sure they knew the truth . . . I'd made up my mind. We all felt—we *knew*—this was the end of an era.

And with every ending is a new beginning.

I'll be forever grateful for my time in *Dreamgirls*. That show offered some of the most extraordinary, wonderful experiences of my life, not to mention some of the most difficult and testing.

And I wouldn't take any of it back.

But, like any true Diva, I know when to make an exit. The next day I hopped a flight to Hollywood, auditioned for *V*, and got the job.

I'd see Michael Bennett one last time. And I had to hand it to him, everything was brilliantly staged to the very end.

The last time I saw him, it was almost over. I went to that famous apartment, the scene of so many exciting parties. Now, those days seemed so long ago. Looking back on them, I seemed like such a child. I'd loved every moment of those parties—the excitement and glitz had been intoxicating. Yet now, in the face of sickness and death, it all seemed so meaningless.

What really mattered was right in front of me: *the truth*. Michael was dying, and there was the youthful realization that life is fleeting, and I needed to appreciate every moment.

There was Michael, God bless him, proud until the end. He was so sick and emaciated. He looked so small and almost childlike in his beautiful bed, lying on the soft white cotton sheets, surrounded by mounds of expensive white pillows. The white, gauzy curtains gave the room a romantic feeling as they fluttered softly in the slightest breeze.

Even as he was dying, there was an air of "production" to Michael.

I entered the room alone. He looked at me. "Oh," he said dismissively. "It's you." But his eyes said something more. He gazed at me with that same Michael look I knew so well. So many emotions passing over his face—anger, exhaustion, pride.

That is when I saw something else, something I could never have understood in the midst of the *Dreamgirls* chaos. Affection. Beneath that tough exterior, and the complex personality, he actually *liked* me. Maybe not me as a person, but my talent. He liked, respected, and ultimately loved that part of me. Under his direction I'd forever be known as the Tony-nominated actress he'd discovered. I'd be the woman who brought his vision to the stage.

My talent had been integral to his "Michael Bennett Presents" life.

This man was fearless with his work. He broke new ground. He went with his gut, doing things other people thought were impossible, nurturing a show no one believed in. He broke the fourth wall, oversaw the creation of sound and sets, and choreographed it all, helping to create an emotionally charged script unlike any the world had ever seen.

In that moment, I know we were thinking the same thing. *We'd been part of something spectacular.* We'd been part of something *revolutionary*. We'd both taken part—*I could see it in his eyes*—in something that would live beyond us both. He was leaving this world, but he was leaving behind a great legacy. And I was part of that legacy.

We talked for a little bit. We talked about stuff that didn't mean anything, just empty words fluttering right along with those curtains. When I left, I knew it would be the last time I saw him.

I wasn't angry. I didn't want to cry, either. What I felt was deep, intense sadness. And hope. Hope that the next world would bring him something he'd never quite found in this one . . . a soothing hand to stroke the hair of that pained little boy he'd kept inside him and tell him *everything was going to be all right*.

I learned another important Diva lesson that day, just a simple word, yet one that I'd never fully understood until that moment.

Forgiveness.

14

A Diva Takes Risks

$\mathcal{L}$eaving a hit Broadway show, especially at the peak of success, was a risk.

But sometimes you have to take the leap. I knew it was time. I'd performed the show over a thousand times, and I needed to move on. As much as I loved her, I couldn't spend the rest of my life playing Deena.

A lot of people were confused by my decision. Leaving a hit Broadway show was something few actors do. But I had to go with my gut, and I did, and now I know it was the right decision.

Just like the men and women who came before me, my Diva-in-training friends, you must *never be afraid to take a risk.* What is the worst that can happen? You'll get a no. And a no won't kill you. In fact, *the no will make you stronger.*

I was never afraid to take those risks.

Part of the reason I am able to continue in the industry is my determination. I refused to rest on my laurels and never took anything for granted. An old Hollywood saying goes, "You're only as good as your last movie." That could easily be interpreted as your last TV show, hit song, or appearance. So don't be afraid to take that risk, no matter how far along you are in your life or in your career. It is never too late to try again.

Take the risk that *you will make it this time*.

Of course, leaving *Dreamgirls* was a huge risk. But I knew it was a risk worth taking.

I still wasn't afraid to put myself out there. One of the hardest transitions to make was playing an iconic character such as Deena, then asking producers and casting directors to see me in a whole new way. It wasn't easy, but I stuck it out. All it takes is one yes. As for the rejections, well, that's part of the game. As I've said, a no might make you stronger. Those ups and downs are part of this game we call life, and you've got to play the game or there is no reason to wake up in the morning. Just like my aunt Mabel, at some point you have to get yourself out that door and into the front seat of that car.

Remember that Diva rule: *life is for living . . . so live!*

That determination paid off. In the years following *Dreamgirls*, I've spent more days on television sets than I can remember. There were seventy-one episodes of *It's a Living,* where I was cast to replace a white actress by the name of Ann Jillian, who left the show after a diagnosis of breast cancer. The producers decided to integrate the cast and I played Ginger St. James. They let me choose a name for my character. Secret? Ginger was short for Virginia. I chose Ginger because the character was feisty, and I wanted something the complete opposite of her conservative upbringing. Her parents wanted a Virginia, and they got a Ginger, like it or not.

I *loved* working on that show!

There were other parts. I was on *Wonder Woman* with Lynda Carter, who was a joy to work with: on *Falcon Crest* and *New Attitude*. *New Attitude* was a groundbreaking series. It starred Phyllis Stickney and me as sisters running a neighborhood beauty salon with a cast that included a young Larenz Tate. I remember telling him, "You are going to be a heartthrob Larenz, just wait." I was right.

That show was a gift to me from producers George Jackson and Doug McHenry, with my old friend Ralph Farquhar as writer. Groundbreaking can also be backbreaking, not to mention ego shaking. But I never once stopped and said, "Now I get to quit trying." There were more and different roads to pave.

Even years later, after I'd proven I could make the transition from Broadway back to Hollywood, I still put myself out there as an actress. But there has always been more to me than my acting, and at this point I found myself even more drawn to political activism. Perhaps taking that leap with *Dreamgirls* showed me a reserve of strength I wasn't fully aware that I had, and now I wanted to use that strength to make the world a better place.

Coming back to LA, I felt a strong drive to get involved in something beyond myself. I had also started dating someone with political aspirations, but few connections, and I hoped to help him make contacts. Those things combined made my plunge into the world of politics almost inevitable. Sometimes, my Diva friends, the world will lead you exactly where you need to go. What I soon found was that activism made me feel just as whole as being an actress.

In 1989, Tom Bradley, the mayor of Los Angeles, had supported the forming of an organization of young black men and women who he felt could make a lasting impression on the city of Los Angeles. He invited me to be a part of this group, which would change my life. Our mission as the YBP, or Young Black Professionals, would be to carry on the legacy of change for the better. We were all very involved in our careers and our communities. All of us understood the power of education, unity, and politics. As a group, the Young Black Professionals were awarded the state's highest honor for our work in the US census. We developed a community campaign that got attention and responses from the community and led to even greater positive developments in South Central LA.

As we worked to understand more the importance of policy making, I'd become enamored with a new politician. He was forward-thinking, refreshing, and I had a gut feeling that he could be the next president of the United States, even though no one knew him. I'd followed his career and had strong hopes for the governor of Arkansas, Bill Clinton.

YBP wanted to organize a fund-raiser for Mr. Clinton, but we didn't want it to be the same old "chicken in the basement of a church" event. We wanted something that was a reflection of us. When I was asked to host—well, there was no need to ask twice. I was truly honored.

We reached out to Kenny G, who provided the entertainment in a brand-new hotel in downtown LA, and the event sold out. The fund-raiser was the last Mr. Clinton would have before he got the Democratic nomination for president. He'd get the presidential nomination the next day and be well on his way to being our next president. I was thrilled to be a part of that historic journey. Sometimes, you've just got to believe!

As the event host I had to be on hand for the Secret Service sweep. I had come straight from a set to make it in time and was all dolled up. The place was a madhouse with the Secret Service doing sweeps of the area, and the night did not start well. I'll never forget. The moment I entered, a Secret Service agent appeared. "Who's the organizer?" he asked briskly.

"She is," said one of my friends, pointing to me.

The agent gave me a quick once-over with a slight smirk. "No," he said. "Who's the *real* organizer?"

I tried to hide my shock. "I *am* the real organizer," I said, my head held high, before breezing past him. I was hurt, but I told myself I am hosting a fund-raiser for the man I believe will be leading our country, and I refuse to let some petty, narrow-minded man mess it up for me. This was an important evening.

We were directed to the back room where we'd welcome the guest of honor before his official appearance. When Bill and Hillary appeared, they were charming and greeted us all kindly, already two political pros. I would meet President Bill Clinton many times in the future and always find him to be a gentleman.

As soon as the Clintons had moved, whom should I see

right behind them? Harry Thomason, whom I knew to be one-half of the production team behind the hit show *Designing Women*. I was a big fan of the show and had seen his image several times in magazines and on TV. I would find out that he and his wife, Linda Bloodworth-Thomason, the other half of the producing team, were huge supporters of the Clintons from the beginning and fully believed in the governor of Arkansas as much as I did.

Maybe it was the way that Secret Service man had looked me up and down and the sudden need to own some of the power he'd *attempted* to take away from me . . . but suddenly I knew what I had to do. As soon as the Clintons had moved on to greet others, I went straight for Mr. Thomason.

"Mr. Thomason?" I said. "Why is it that after six years on the air, you do not have *one black woman* on *Designing Women*? The show takes place in Atlanta, and all the women are white. Now, c'mon, we both know that's not very realistic. Here's what I think: you need a black woman on that show. The Anthony character needs a woman. He needs a wife to stand beside him, and I should play the part."

Mr. Thomason was a bit taken aback. He smiled at me a bit uneasily. "And who exactly, are you?" he asked.

"Sheryl Lee Ralph. I'm hosting this event tonight and I am a friend of Tim Flack." Tim Flack was a well-respected casting director, now at CBS.

"Well, have Tim Flack call my people and maybe we'll schedule you a meeting sometime."

The classic Hollywood answer: not much of an answer at all. At that point I'd really begun to own and develop my Diva strengths . . . and I wouldn't take his challenge to me as a *no*.

Two days later I had an appointment at his office.

When I walked in, Mr. Thomason was not there. Instead, his wife, Linda Bloodworth-Thomason, entered the room like a force of energy. She looked me up and down. "So, you're the woman who accosted my husband."

"Yes," I said. "And you're the woman who is going to hire me."

A moment passed, and she broke into a smile.

I was cast as Etienne Toussaint Bouvier, a Vegas showgirl turned Anthony's wife, for two episodes. They kept me after the second episode, and then after that. The part was one of my favorites. Etienne was hilarious and over-the-top. In one of my favorite scenes ever, I got to play the Scarlett O'Hara role in *Gone With the Wind*. I would never have imagined in my early twenties a time when I'd get to parody on television such a famous white character, not to mention slap one of the main characters of *Designing Women* across the face and watch her tumble down the stairs as I bellowed, "As God is my witness, I'll never be hungry again!"

True, it was a *dream sequence*, but still, that was a scene you would never have seen when I'd started out. Times were changing and I was in the middle of the mix.

To this day, I'm glad I went over to Mr. Thomason and told him what I'd been thinking all those years. After six seasons, it was about time that show had a black female character, and I was proud to play her and give her life. And sure, Mr. Thomason could have said no to me, or something far worse. But that was a risk I was willing to take.

A Diva will walk right up to the man, grab him by the collar, and say, "Hire me. I'm what you need."

Divatude is taking risks. Divatude is going with your guts. And sometimes you'll make mistakes—believe me, I've made plenty—but *mistake* is another word for *experience*. Besides, a Diva knows that *no* today can be a *yes, ma'am* tomorrow!

Just wait and see . . . eventually someone will say yes. And all it takes is *one yes*.

And when you finally get that yes—and you *will*, my Diva sisters—what do you do next? Sit back and gloat? Of course not! A Diva knows a *yes* is when the real work begins.

Around this time, visionary film director Charles Burnett, the legend behind the national treasure *Killer of Sheep*, approached me. I believe Charles is one of the "greatest filmmakers you might not have heard of." I'd always admired his work and was thrilled when he wanted me to play a role in his newest film, *To Sleep With Anger*.

I was immediately drawn in by the title. When I was growing up, my parents always told me that going to sleep angry—both literally and figuratively—could ruin a marriage and destroy families. They weren't just talking about at the end of the day, but in general. Danny Glover had already been cast as the lead. Charles thought I was perfect to play the part of Linda, the bourgeois daughter-in-law. Charles wanted a darker-skinned black woman "to represent wealth and intelligence." I later found out that even though he had made up his mind, he'd had to fight for me to be cast.

One of the producers thought I was "too black" for the role. This producer made it known that he wanted someone more Halle Berry–ish. And if taking issue with the shade of my skin wasn't enough, he had other issues with me: "She has big legs."

I'd had people take issue with my lips before, but my legs? This was a new one. A version of my leg had been used in the iconic *Dreamgirls* poster, yet this guy didn't find them satisfactory? In the end, Charles wouldn't back down. "I want Sheryl Lee Ralph," he said until he got his way. Unfortunately, this wouldn't be the last of his battles. That same producer regularly voiced his opinions, and they were often in direct opposition to Charles's magnificent vision. In other words, this set had constant drama.

I'll never forget the last night of shooting. We were doing a simple "reversal" of one of my best scenes. A *reversal* shot is one from the opposite side or direction of the prior shot, to tell the story from both sides. When I got to the set, I was informed by the producer that my shot was going to be dropped. *There was no time for it,* he said. This scene was important for my character and the movie as a whole. When you've worked so hard to make it as an actress and someone makes a last-minute decision to cut your pivotal moment—well, I was discouraged and hurt to say the least. This was my big shot, *literally.*

I left the set and headed back to my dressing room. My head was spinning as I removed my wardrobe and packed my things. I was going home. I tried to stay strong and fight back the tears. Just as I was about to open the door, someone was knocking. There stood Danny Glover. Besides starring in the film, Danny also had a producer credit. He looked at my face and immediately knew something was up. "Where are you going?" he asked.

"Home," I told him.

"We can't finish the movie without you. Wait. Is this because we aren't shooting your reversal?"

I could only nod my head yes, and just like that I burst into tears. I was so embarrassed, but I couldn't help it. "Sheryl Lee," he said in a determined voice, "don't worry. You'll get your shot."

As much as I believe in staying strong, my fellow Divas, at times your feelings will overwhelm you. And just as your strength is beautiful, so is your vulnerability. Your authentic emotions are part of what makes you unique and extraordinary. Sometimes you have just got to be real and let your feelings show.

Danny took care of everything and I got my shot. I believe that shot helped me win the Independent Spirit Award for Best Supporting Actress, which is the indie film version of the Oscars. Danny won for Best Lead Actor and Charles for Best Director, his screenplay going on to win at Sundance and Cannes. *To Sleep With Anger* was a success.

The Independent Spirit Awards are meant to honor those actors and filmmakers who—against all odds—make movies outside the studio system. While the main purpose of many big-budget movies is to make money, independent films are still a place where artists can explore their craft, oftentimes without studio support or money. Frequently, actors will gladly take less pay or no pay to work with the directors they admire and play parts that excite them. The actual Independent Spirit Award is an albatross on a pole trying to fly with a shoestring, and this is a pretty good description of the challenges involved in low-budget, independent filmmaking.

My nomination was bittersweet. The shoot had been difficult. Despite the trials, winning the award was thrilling. When they called my name, I was shocked. As I headed for the stage, I felt a rush of emotion. I looked out at that crowd of gifted people, many of whom were (and still are) fighting the odds to make good films in a world where box office sales are often placed far above story, characters, and, *yes,* acting. Many in this community are fighting to preserve their vision. They want to tell the cinematic truth in their own meaningful way, and they don't want a studio to tell them how to do it.

I felt an urge to do the same.

I thanked those who had voted for me, my cast, and my director. I went on to say how honored I was because I knew how hard it was for black actresses "to win" since there were so few roles for us to play. I shared what was said to me in my first big studio meeting after leaving *Dreamgirls* and returning to Hollywood when the head of casting had said he didn't know what to "do" with a beautiful, talented black girl. That I couldn't play opposite Tom Cruise–caliber leading men because no audience would want to see that kind of couple kiss. Now I went on to say how it was time for the industry to get to know the black actress and begin to write for her. *We are here too,* I said, *and we deserve to work too.*

I received a shocked but enthusiastic round of applause and went back to my seat with the satisfaction of knowing that maybe—just maybe—one of those young, gifted directors, writers, or producers would take my words to heart. Maybe for their next movie they'd choose to cast a talented black actress, whatever her shade of black might be.

The handsome Andy Garcia was next on the mike. "Sheryl Lee Ralph," he said with a respectful grin, "I'll kiss you on-screen *anytime*."

The next day my entire speech and I were on the front page of *Variety*.

As I said, a *yes* can be satisfying. And eventually you will open some doors. Unfortunately, some of them will only open so far.

Along with the great parts, there were great disappointments. *Randall and Juliet,* for instance, an American remake of a successful French film called *Romuald et Juliette,* where I'd been cast in the juicy lead role opposite Richard Dreyfuss. He played a wealthy, conservative executive who falls in love with my five children and me. The picture was set up at Disney with its original French director Coline Serreau, the woman who also created the original *Three Men and a Baby*.

Richard dropped out on the first day of rehearsal after having issues with the director. Almost immediately, they'd begun yelling and Coline had stormed off the set. "Did you hear her?" he asked me. Without waiting for an answer, he left too.

I stood there and watched the whole project disappear right in front of my eyes. Following his exit, we had a leading lady, but we still needed a leading man.

The studio immediately tried to recast the role. Ted Danson came in to read with me, but I don't think the magic was there. Robert De Niro and I had made magic together in *Mistress,* but someone at Disney just couldn't or wouldn't see him in the role.

I prayed that the project would go on, but the months passed and so did the project. The material was timely and wonderful, but no one was quite sure how to make it move forward. The door had been opened to me and almost immediately shut in my face. Still, there was no time to sit and weep. I had to find a new way in.

Black women still have a hard time getting in, getting cast, and I guarantee at times even now are told they aren't the "right shade of black." But does that mean you go away silently and take it? Not a Diva like you or me, my friends. We owe it to ourselves—and those who will come after us—to speak up.

You have to be willing to fight for what you want, my lovely Divas. And I do not mean taking off your high heels and earrings. *Absolutely not.* A real Diva can be tough and stand up for herself without compromising herself. A real Diva treats others the way she would like to be treated. Even as times change, you must remember where you came from or you'll get lost trying to figure out where you are going.

Of course, there will be disappointments along the way. But even in the most difficult of times, there are the beautiful moments.

Without a doubt, my time on *Moesha* had both.

15

Mo Diva, Mo Problems

When Ralph Farquhar called me to say that he *had my next series,* I wasn't surprised but appreciative. I'd known Ralph since I was nineteen years old. I first met Ralph during my screen test for *A Piece of the Action.*

I'll never forget walking onto the Warner Bros. lot for my screen test, and seeing so many young black faces. All I could think was "Wow!" Every black Hollywood actor and actress in their teens and early twenties seemed to be there, and that was a rare sight in those days. There was a buzz of excitement, and it felt good.

Ralph Farquhar and his friend Peter Wise had walked right over to me and introduced themselves. The attention immediately set me at ease. Years later, Ralph would tell me that he remembered looking at me thinking, *Whoa, who is that? That girl is something special.* Thinking back, I can't help but smile. We were all so eager and brimming with hope. We knew that, as young actors, we were embarking on a journey that would be difficult for all of us. There would be pitfalls and mistakes, but we had what it took to survive.

Both those men went on to great careers, Ralph as a prolific writer/producer who has opened the door for many young actors and producers, and Peter Wise as a successful casting director. All these years later, I'm lucky to count them among my friends.

So when Ralph called to say he was executive producer of a show with the perfect part for me, I was all ears. "You'll love the character, Sheryl Lee. The show is great. You'll play the stepmother and voice of reason. The star is this bright young performer named Brandy. You know her?"

"Of course!" I told him. I was thrilled. I had followed Brandy's career, and I thought she had a great voice and personality to match. Seeing a talented young black girl being herself—braids and all—filled me with joy.

Brandy reminded me of my early days auditioning and trying to make a place for myself in Hollywood. I remembered wearing braids early in my career, and a director asking me, "Can't you find a more *natural* hairstyle?" My response: "Natural for whom?"

Seeing Brandy made me feel good. I had to fight to wear my braids, just as the incomparable actress Rosalind Cash had to fight for her beautiful dreadlocks, and now Brandy could be famous *with* her braids. In some way, I felt as though we had helped pave the pathway for her freedom of expression as a person and artist. I was always cheering for her success. Brandy's success felt like a triumph for me. How could I *not* feel good for her? A new day was dawning and I had a *front-row seat*.

That Ralph was asking me to participate in a show full of young black faces—a show that we could only dream about when we'd met so many years ago—filled me with a sense of accomplishment.

Moesha was like coming full circle and coming home at the same time.

In so many ways, *Moesha* was a historically important show, one of the first television programs to bring a cast of middle-class black people into the average living room and show them loving each other and their communities. This show didn't back down from real issues: drugs, teenage pregnancy, broken homes.

All those themes were there in the final episode.

Moesha ended with a showdown when the Frank character protects his "son" Dorian, who had become involved with a dangerous drug dealer. At the same time, Moesha finds out she is pregnant and runs off with her high school sweetheart Q, leaving the guy who truly loves her, Hakeem, wondering what just happened. In what would become the end of the *Moesha* series, a devastated Frank is left alone. He has no one to turn to, especially since my character, Dee, has mysteriously disappeared . . . to Jamaica.

The audience was left with loose ends, unfinished plotlines, and unanswered questions. This was a disappointing end to a show that had broken so many barriers and been loved by so many. A show that was brave enough to be ahead of the times.

Moesha deserved better. And so did I.

Moesha dealt with real-life issues and was one of the first shows to bring the reality of a "new" kind of family to the small screen. Dee was a stepmother coming in to raise her husband's two children. Just as in real life, it wasn't always easy for her.

To this day, mothers come up and thank me for showing them how to deal with and love their stepchildren.

In some ways, the issues within the cast mirrored the issues of the real world. As is often the case, the stepmother finds it easier to bond with the younger child. As for the older child, it saddened me—and still does—that Brandy and I did not end up having the relationship I'd hoped for.

Looking back, my time on that show had its ups and downs. There were wonderful moments, and I was pleased that so many viewers found my character, Dee, inspiring. Dee loved Frank dearly and ended up loving his children even more. Even though Dee was a stepmother, my character was voted one of "America's Favorite TV Moms," which was a great honor.

At the same time, there were some really low moments. Working with a cast of young people as one of the few adults put me face-to-face with teenage Hollywood hormones.

I love young people. Just like all young people, young actors make mistakes too. That's human. And let me tell you, I know this from personal experience because I made quite a few mistakes of my own.

Kids can be rude and disrespectful. They can say things that shouldn't be said . . . to *anyone*. They can hurt you in ways you didn't think were possible. But as the adult, you must resist the temptation to hurt them back because they are young and—for the most part—*not fully in their right minds*. They say the front lobe of the brain, the part that helps you make decisions, is the last to develop. So whether they like it or not, and as much as they might lash out, you must continue to guide young people with love. And, trust me, as a mother of two, it ain't easy!

There is no point in my looking back on those *Moesha* years with anger or bitterness. But the reality was, at times I was disrespected by the younger cast members. Ultimately the good times certainly outweighed the bad, but it still *hurt*.

When sudden stardom and success come your way, having good guidance is *key*. Real Divas learn to handle success with grace because they have good role models to help and guide them. Unfortunately, many young actors lose themselves when they become successful because they have no real foundation or sense of self. They have no real guidance.

Often, young Hollywood stars are surrounded by people who are paid to say yes. *Yes, you look good! Yes, you're right! Yes, have another drink. Yes, I'll take the rap, yes, yes, yes!* And when you lose perspective on reality . . . well, you are bound to lose yourself.

My daily goal was to do my job well and go home. I had a life to lead and children to raise. When young, inexperienced people are calling the shots from the podium of success and popularity, the environment is ripe to become chaotic.

During long, late lunch breaks, young cast members were obviously enjoying themselves behind closed dressing-room doors. The shooting schedule would run over by hours, and *that makes it hard on everybody*. As an adult cast member, I had a family waiting for me at home, and that kind of disregard for other people on the set was not appropriate, not to mention *unprofessional*.

I had to stand up for myself and others on the crew who had families and lives they needed to get home to. The younger cast members would not always take kindly to my honesty. In some ways, they began to see me as the wicked stepmother who was *ruining* their good time. With their handlers being paid to keep them happy, they were often told their feelings of injustice were perfectly acceptable. Or, in other cases, their attitude was simply ignored.

Let's be clear, the show was called *Moesha,* not *Moesha's Mom.* What Brandy wanted—Brandy got. She was young and had been thrust into the bright light of fame. I'm sure it was confusing and overwhelming, it had been for me.

It is always the straw that breaks the camel's back, something seemingly small. Hair is always important for women, especially black women . . . but it certainly didn't seem big enough to make a TV show combust. But when you are a young star spending all your time on a set, and you have teenage insecurity, and reality is no longer something you completely comprehend . . . well, a hairstyle might be just the thing to set it all off!

I got my hair braided. Braids have always been my summertime hairstyle of choice, and it was a nice change. The show resumed shooting in late summer and I went to work with my hair braided and pulled back in a ponytail.

At first Brandy seemed to love my hair, saying that we looked like twins. But behind the scenes I guess it was another story. She wasn't happy at all with my wearing braids. According to her, the braids were her style, *her thing.*

Never mind that I'd had to fight for my own braids decades earlier. The great actress Cicely Tyson fought for her braids, the model Naomi Sims made braids a fashion statement, and Cleopatra used hers to woo Caesar into submission. Generations of women opened the door for her to wear braids proudly on national television.

None of that mattered. The producers knew they had to make the star happy. They asked me nicely to take out the braids. I refused. They told me not as nicely to take out the braids. I refused. They then offered to donate $25,000 to my charity and pay to have a wig handmade for me in the hairstyle of my choice. At that point, I figured I'd made my point and said okay.

But the damage had already been done. When a hairstyle causes such misery and pain for someone, you know things are reaching a low point. The show was no longer about the audience or the plot or the characters, but was fueled by backstage drama.

If you know anything about me by now, my Divalicious friends, you know I don't have time for petty drama.

The relationship I had always hoped to have with Brandy seemed to sadly disappear. By the end of my run on the show, the set had become toxic for me . . . and when I am in a toxic environment, I make the healthy choice and get out of there as quickly as I can.

So, yes, I chose to leave a successful show. My own sanity matters more to me than any paycheck. Being able to look myself in the mirror and know I've been true to myself matters even more.

Distance gives perspective. Years later I received a call from one of the young male cast members in the show. "I've gotten my act together, Miss Sheryl," he said. "I was wrong. And I just wanted to say I'm sorry for how I acted sometimes. I'm really sorry."

I told him all was forgiven. All *was* and *is* forgiven.

When I heard of Brandy's troubles with her car accident, I

cut off anyone I heard gossiping about her. I cared about her and all I could think was *that poor girl*. Nobody should ever have to go through something that tragic, and she must have been in so much pain. All these years later, despite everything that had happened, I was *still worried about her feelings*.

Moesha was full of rough times, but it was also full of wonderful life-changing moments too. I have held on to those moments tightly and chalk up the less pleasant ones to this thing we call *experience*.

Above all, this is what I hold on to: I was blessed to have had such a long run on another successful show. There is no point in anger. Anger will hold you back, my Diva friends. Anger isn't healthy or productive, and it doesn't look good on your face.

I certainty won't allow anything to ruin my good looks. *Can I get an amen?*

Recently I ran into Brandy at a wedding. The moment she saw me, she hugged me tightly and started crying. "I was just a kid," she said. "I didn't know any better. You always wanted the best for me. I understand that now."

I looked at the strong, beautiful woman she had become and cried right along with her.

A show like *Moesha*—depicting real black teenagers with real positive lives—proves just how far we've come as black people.

Unfortunately, some people may have forgotten to count their many blessings. More than that, they might have forgotten or didn't know how hard those who came before them *worked* and *sacrificed* to make these amazing opportunities a reality for all of us.

And their real responsibility is to do that for the next generation.

This is why, when I think of my early days in television, I hold people like Roxie, Sherman, and Ralph close to my heart. I would never be who I am if it hadn't been for Virginia Capers, Rosalind Cash, Beverly Todd, and the countless others I had the opportunity to work and grow with. These men and women taught me the value of *appreciation*.

Just as the transition from *Dreamgirls* to Hollywood was difficult, the one I had to make when *Moesha* ended wasn't easy either. But I survived and thrived. Other parts were waiting for me. Other movies and television shows. Other passions to pursue.

Above all, I had people who loved me and all the love in the world to give back to them . . . and no TV show in the world could match that.

16

A Diva Looks Back . . . and Forward

I wouldn't take anything back. Not from *Dreamgirls* or *Moesha,* and not from the many experiences after. Following *Dreamgirls* would come my top-ten dance hit "In the Evening," numerous roles on sitcoms, parts in movies. I'd work regularly in the years to come. As a black woman in an industry where white is considered highly preferable—well, I take extraordinary pride in my career.

But a career won't keep you warm at night. All the awards in the world—while incredibly gratifying—are nothing but cold metal at the end of the day. What has kept me going is something far bigger and more important.

Soon after my experiences in *Dreamgirls,* I began to fully feel the aftereffects of what I'd seen in New York. All those beautiful, vibrant men, many of whose lives were just getting started, wasting away to nothing or, even worse, just dropping dead. For every song I sang, there was another they never had a chance to write. For every dance move, line of dialogue, elegant costume, gorgeous lyric, there were the countless ones that had been lost forever. There were families—mothers, fathers, siblings, lovers—for whom a piece of their souls had suddenly been torn away.

When my angel Tom Eyen, the man who created the original concept and idea for the show that eventually became *Dreamgirls* became sick, my heart sank. He had always been such a big supporter of mine, from that first moment I met him backstage and he pitched an *unnamed future hit show with a part for me*. I knew that he loved me in a special way. He wanted me to find love. "Always follow your heart. Always," he would tell me. "Always remember who you are and that you are special."

Tom was always giving me little pearls of advice. Sometimes I didn't have the slightest idea what he was saying, but one day during his illness he said to me, "When you start doing your good work, remember that you are Audrey Hepburn and not Marilyn Monroe." Confused? Well, so was I. I chalked it up to dementia.

Not until years later did I understand exactly what he meant. I had a different calling.

I knew how blessed I was, and I wanted to do something to make the world better. In the footsteps of my grandfather, I knew "to whom much is given, much is expected." My community was important to me, especially the children. Children are a gift to society and must be cared for as the extraordinary beings they are. I had friends who felt the same way, Pauletta and Denzel Washington. I had starred in one of my favorite movies, *The Mighty Quinn,* with Denzel Washington—and to answer your question, *yes, he is as wonderful as everyone says.* I mean, what a dream role! People ask me to this day what it was like to work with Denzel, and I tell them all the same thing: *It was better than you think.*

But what made him truly remarkable was something beyond his perfect face. It was his big heart.

Together Denzel, Pauletta, and I founded the Los Angeles Children's Toy Drive. We felt that there would always be those children in certain communities who—for a myriad of reasons—would fall between the cracks and not receive a toy for Christmas. We wanted to fill the gap. Every year, with the help of our star friends, we put on a party and toy drive for the children of South Central.

Louil Silas was a young record producer of that time, and he introduced us to a hot new group who he said would become stars to sing at our first party. They were still unknown at the time and went by the name New Edition. New indeed! They were raw, young talents and could not have been nicer.

That first year we raised a mountain of toys. I'll never forget the many Christmas holidays we delivered toys to some of the most dangerous neighborhoods in LA.

We weren't afraid of Imperial Courts or Nickerson Gardens, though maybe we should have been. But we followed our political godmother, Maxine Waters, where she was not afraid to go, and so we chose to be unafraid and go too. In the mid to late eighties gangs ruled many of those hoods, and colors identified the gangs. Red was for Bloods and blue was for Crips. Just wearing the wrong color in the wrong neighborhood could get you shot. So what was I thinking other than *It's Christmas and I'm Santa's helper!* when I dressed in red from top to bottom. No problem . . . until it became a problem in one of the hoods we visited.

As soon as the limo pulled up in that neighborhood and we started to get out of the car, we were met by a group of tough-looking men leaning up against a wall. They took one look and went on high alert. The guys just glared at me, probably not even noticing the famous actor I was with.

Denzel was right to be worried.

God bless Denzel. He told me to get back in the limo in a manner that made me know not to ask why. Denzel and I had a brother/sister kind of relationship . . . we argued at the drop of a hat. I knew not to argue at that moment.

We all got back in the car as Denzel took time to quickly regroup. He exhaled and got out and strode over to the guys with that walk of his. What was going on in the minds of the men up against the wall I can only imagine. But I watched Denzel walk right up to them and introduce himself with all of the confidence of an alpha male. It was almost surreal, this huge movie star just hanging out with the brothas on the neighborhood wall! He talked with them for a while, then walked back to the car and barked, "Give me the camera!"

He walked back over to the wall and took pictures with them. The whole crazy scene ended with handshakes and thin smiles. Denzel nodded at the guys and headed back to the car.

"Okay, Sheryl," he said. "I want you to get out of the car and walk quickly—and I mean quickly—into the building. Don't look around, don't talk to anyone. Move fast and everything will be all right."

That's just what we did, and everything was fine. Better than fine. When we saw the smiles on the faces of the children, everything was great. Those kids were so thrilled with the presents they didn't care anything about the colors of my clothes.

Years later, I was stopped by a young man who asked me if I remembered giving away toys in the hood at Christmas.

How could I forget those Christmases? He smiled broadly and said, "I got one of those toys. It meant a lot to me, that you guys cared about us enough to come to our neighborhood. And guess what? I have a job now."

He made me cry. You never know the ways, my lovely Divas, in which you might touch a life.

I was active in other charities—YBP, which helped with the Clintons' fund-raiser, and the United Negro College Fund. I enjoyed working in all of them. But something kept nagging at me. Tom Eyen, Michael Peters, Michael Bennett, and so many of the other men in our original Broadway company—those men that had tragically been lost to AIDS. I couldn't forget how many of them suffered in silence under stigma and shame.

Then I realized the truth was right there, it had been the whole time. What Michael Peters had seen that Thursday on the street, his graceful dancer's body hobbled by disease—that *I* had to break that silence and bring attention to the many men we had lost. I had the backing and adoration of the gay community, and many friends and acquaintances I knew who could help. And those who weren't sure, well, I'd convince them.

It was clear to me, this wasn't just about those wonderful gay men. Sex had led to death, and straight men and women couldn't be far behind. I had to do something, for all of them.

* * *

It was the end of the eighties and men had and were still dropping like flies. People were still afraid of AIDS. You saw it on their faces, literally. Many people wore those strange purple masks to "protect" themselves. Their fear was right there on their faces like a sad, misguided armor that won't protect you from anything, especially not the truth.

As for those who were dying? Well, sometimes you'd go to the hospital to visit your friend, but there was no hospital bed for him. Often you would find him out in the hallway, pushed up against the wall, truly dying for help. But there was no help for them. No human touch. No hugs and, in so many cases, no love. Fear rendered people silent and at times inhumane. I had been taught to believe that *there but for the grace of God go I.* So how could I turn my back as my friends suffered and died?

I was determined to break the deadly silence and get a conversation started. Some people told me that it would hurt my career to align myself with such a controversial disease and *those people.* Others said that maybe—if I were a *big* star like Elizabeth Taylor—it might be worth it . . . but I was just me, *so why take the risk?* But nothing hurt me more than when some-one looked at me and said, "God will find no favor with you."

More often than I can count or even remember, more days and moments and times than you'd think humanly possible, I would end the day with one simple action.

I cried.

How could they think that the God I believed in—my God—could be so cruel? The God I was raised to believe in was not the kind to turn away, not see—or even more ludi-crous, *condone* the suffering of others. People wouldn't under-stand or listen when I told them that my friends had been good and kind men. Not to mention somebody's son, husband, and father. They were all loving children of God.

Besides, any community with so many members who could help you with your wig, weave, weft, and wardrobe problems . . . well, *those were men* who deserved to be appreciated and remembered!

I founded the Diva Foundation in 1990 as a nonprofit organization to raise awareness and serve as a memorial to the many friends I had lost to AIDS. The organization focuses on generating resources and spreading HIV/AIDS awareness and the threat I believe it is especially posing to women and children. We talked about difficult questions you have to ask to protect yourself. *What is your status?* And I'm not talking loan status, I mean HIV. *Do you sleep with men or women? Do you use intravenous drugs?* And, of course, *have you been tested?* To that one, many people answered honestly, and the answer was no. They were afraid, they would tell me. It was too difficult a process to go through alone. Eventually, my husband and I created a place in which couples can get the answers they need together, *www.testtogether.org*.

I took my message everywhere from high schools to senior citizen homes, and, yes, churches too. I've handed out condoms at every single engagement.

AIDS does not discriminate, and neither do I.

I produced the first Divas Simply Singing! in 1990. The concept was simple: the light, the mike, and the Diva who would simply sing to piano. And she'd do it *alone,* 'cause we didn't have the money to pay for a band and I believe musicians should always get paid.

This is how the first one happened: I picked up the phone

and called my Diva girlfriends, because I knew they had the stuff to hold an audience's attention with the solitary power of their extraordinary presence. And that is exactly what Debbie Allen, Dianne Reeves, Mary Wilson, Brenda Russell, and Pauletta Washington did.

Over the years, this unique concert brought out some of the greatest voices of our time in so many different areas of entertainment—including my fellow Dreamgirls Loretta Devine, Jennifer Holliday, and Jenifer Lewis—to raise money for AIDS awareness by raising their voices in song.

And we *have* raised money. And with that money made lives better . . . and hopefully even saved some.

In 2010 we celebrated the twentieth Divas Simply Singing! We are now the longest consecutive-running musical HIV/AIDS fund-raiser in the country. We have come together year after year, always hitting the mark of love, tolerance, and acceptance. Divas Simply Singing! continues to serve as a beacon of light for those who have and are fighting the good fight against HIV/AIDS, and I thank my fellow Diva Janet Jackson for writing that first $5,000 check that got us on our way.

The more I traveled across the country speaking about HIV/AIDS, the more I realized that people didn't know or want to know about HIV/AIDS. It seemed to me that as the years had passed, the silence that had surrounded my friends was back again. But in the least expected places—Southern rural towns where the most exciting thing happening was watching the grass grow—women would take me aside and talk in hushed tones. *We got it here,* they told me, *we got that disease here.* A son, a father. Sometimes even a husband.

And just as frequently, eyes downcast, they'd say, "I got it."

Their stories—shame and secrecy—filled me with such sadness. I thought I knew something about AIDS, but right before me the face of the disease was changing and nobody was uttering a word. There was no march on Washington for them.

I knew the people of sub-Saharan Africa were fighting seemingly futilely against AIDS, but right here in America women from all walks of life were suffering in silence from a disease so many of them were afraid to name. They were dying of it, and they were doing it alone.

I knew this: silence equals death. If nobody else was going to do something, then someone had to. And you, my Diva, should—might already be—doing the same in your own way. Using your gifts and voice to make the world better.

I picked up my pen and started writing. I was giving voices to my sisters' stories. I wrote my one-woman show, *Sometimes I Cry,* based on interviews I had done with real women, all who had a unique female perspective and a story to tell. The women you would never expect . . . your mother or neighbor or the girl working behind the counter at the grocery store. I decided to tell their stories for them, and that is just what I did.

I took my show and put it on the road. I performed for anyone who wanted to hear, and some who didn't. From audiences of rowdy students to reserved businessmen, the rich and the poor. Church doors opened slowly to me, but they did open.

I keep up with many of these women whose stories I

performed. And seeing their strength keeps me strong. Precious, LaNell, Julan, Regan, Cathy, Ray, just to name a few. Their hope gives me hope. Giving back brings me joy and satisfaction. A real Diva counts—and shares—her blessings. She wants to leave the world a better place than when she found it.

I know, my Diva friends, you can and will use your power to do the same.

An Epilogue . . .

The Diva's Final Chapter

$\mathcal{M}$y philanthropic work is a blessing. That I continue to work as an actress, that is a blessing too. But the biggest blessing of all? The one that means more than anything else to me? The love of my children and husband.

The kind of unconditional love your family gives you, well, there is nothing more powerful. To be blessed with a husband I believe in—and who believes in me—makes everything worthwhile. Watching my children grow and thrive makes life worth living. Their successes—and knowing I raised them with the same love and confidence my parents gave me—are a blessing. The kind of love they needed to succeed is something powerful beyond words.

And as you know, I am rarely at a loss for words.

Wait, I have one . . . *sacred*. That word says everything.

As for you, my Diva friends, I pray my experiences—mistakes and bad breaks included—have given you inspiration, hope, and comfort.

I hope you've learned there will always be somebody taller or shorter, prettier, smarter, or the opposite. There are all those people . . . and then there is *you*.

And *you*, my dear Diva, are perfect *just the way you are*. God does not make mistakes. You are perfect, and what you choose to do and say with your perfect self, well, that is the key.

I hope that you will learn to wake up in the morning, look in the mirror, and truly love what you see. Life is for the living, my *Divinely Inspired Victoriously Alive* friends. You must live it to the fullest with every beat of your heart.

Every day aboveground is a good day! You are blessed to wake up and put two feet on the floor and take life one step at a time. There will be good times and bad times, true—highs and lows—but, in the end, you must be thankful for them all.

I know I am.

I encourage you to increase your dream quotient, Diva! That's right, dream bigger, honey! And don't waste time feeling bad about having big dreams. Forget that! Feel bad only if— and I know this won't be a problem—you don't work to make those dreams come true.

Open yourself up to receive all the good that is out there for you.

Dress yourself in your dreams and wear them well.

A real Diva knows that every experience she has—the good, the bad, and the breathtakingly beautiful ones—all challenge her to grow and evolve and offer new chapters in her extraordinary life. And a true Diva—*the kind you and I are, my friends*—embraces the unknown journey with fearless hope in her heart.

A true Diva can't wait to turn the next page in her life—to look at that empty, promising space—and fill in the blankness with her own exceptional story.

Acknowledgments

The last course I took as a college student was a writing course, and the professor's name was Cheryl. Upon handing me my final written composition she said, "It's a shame this is your last class, you could be very good at this." She inspired me in that moment and I have never forgotten it. So here I go after all this writing. Thank you, Cheryl.

In labors of love such as the writing of this book I have so many people to thank, and I fear that I might forget someone. So if I do, I ask you to blame it on my mind and not my heart because you know how much I thank you! At times in my life I have been surrounded by angels who revealed themselves unselfishly, pushing me forward and raising me up when I didn't think I could make it. You know who you are and I thank you.

To everyone who encouraged me to write this book, I thank you because I honestly didn't know I had a story to tell. I am so good at telling other people's stories that I tucked my own away, but you saw it. Thank you, E. Lynn Harris. I know you are happy to see me complete this journey as a writer. You told me before you left us, "Diva, this book must be written." I had to fulfill the command. Thank you, Susan Taylor, for taking me on that walk and asking, "Where is the book? What are you waiting for?" Thank you, John Edwards, for looking me squarely in the eyes and asking me, "When are you writing the book?" then quickly telling me, "No, you are writing a book." It wasn't easy digging deep and putting to paper things that I would have liked to forget, but in the end it is written and I thank you for believing in me when I didn't believe in myself.

This book is about celebrating the DIVA—Divinely Inspired Victoriously Alive—person you were meant to be. I encourage you to live a fabulously rich and wonderful life knowing that you are perfect, DIVA, just the way you are. God does not make mistakes, and she knows what she is doing. Let go of the notion that there is something wrong with being a DIVA woman or man. DIVA is an equal opportunity way of living and it should be embraced . . . often. Live Divaliciously and empower yourself to be bodacious, generous, graceful, outrageous, kind, beautiful, over-the-top, and juicy! Live it! Love it! *You* are it!

Last and certainly not least, I would like to thank Maya Sloan for her wonderful contributions to the creation and completion of this book. Thank you for helping me paint my soul with words.